TOM WRIGHT was proprietor of the Old Scotland in F
Leith Walk in Edinburgh for over 30 years. He is no
specialised in Victorian and Edwardian photographs of
collection of negatives and postcards accumulated during this period, this book is a
complete change of direction from his previous books about football.

On leaving school at 15, Tom's first job was in Leith, where he quickly acquired
a great affinity with the Port and its unique atmosphere. An affinity that continues to
this very day.

He is married to wife Liz and has two daughters and four grandchildren.

Tom is also author of *The Golden Years: Hibernian in the Days of the Famous Five*,
Hibernian: From Joe Baker to Turnbull's Tornadoes and co-author of *Crops: The Alex
Cropley Story*.

Glimpses of Times Past

LEITH

TOM WRIGHT

Luath Press Limited
EDINBURGH
www.luath.co.uk

First published 2014
Reprinted 2017

ISBN: 978-1-908373-65-6

The paper used in this book is recyclable.
It is made from low chlorine pulps
produced in a low energy, low emissions
manner from renewable forests.

Printed and bound by
Bell & Bain Ltd., Glasgow

All photographs and postcards used in
the book are from the personal collection
of Tom Wright.

Typeset in 10 point Gill Sans by
3btype.com

CONTENTS

INTRODUCTION

The historic seaport town of Leith has a long and illustrious past. Throughout the years it has survived periods of siege, occupation, famine and plague, and has often been at the forefront of many other colourful and significant events that have help shape Scottish history as we know it. During these turbulent times, however, the port has always succeeded in retaining its own individual sense of identity.

The earliest recorded evidence of a settlement at Leith dates from 1143 confirming that there had been a habitation on both sides of the mouth of what is now known as the Water of Leith for almost a thousand years, but in all probability there would have been a settlement in the area much earlier, possibly before even that of Edinburgh. Almost certainly the Romans would have passed through the area as they travelled between the forts at Cramond and Fisherrow after arriving in Scotland in 80AD. These early settlements, probably consisting of no more than a few dozen primitive dwellings, would have relied almost totally on the sea for their very existence, and it was Leith estuary that would play such a major part in the development of Leith from a small village into the Scotland's leading seaport during the 17th and 18th centuries.

Leith had always been regarded as Edinburgh's trading gateway to the world, a fact not lost on its city fathers who had long been envious of the port's flourishing prosperity and worldwide reputation. In 1329, King Robert the Bruce, in one of his last acts before his death that same year, handed Edinburgh control of the harbour at Leith to the great dismay of the occupants of the town. The animosity between the two increased even further when Sir Robert Logan, who was then almost bankrupt, sold the superiority of his lands surrounding the south side of the shore to Edinburgh in 1398, allowing the city almost total control of trade in the port.

Despite the continuing acrimony, Leith came into its own during the middle ages. Although severely disadvantaged by the shallow depth of water, particularly at low tide, further redevelopment of the harbour paved the way for significant increase in foreign trade. This increase also led to a growth in shipbuilding, particularly after the construction of a swing bridge at Sandport Street in the 1780s that allowed much larger craft access further upriver. The increase in shipbuilding also had a huge impact on the ancillary trades such as sail making, rope manufacture, the import of timber, and a rise in the number of general merchants that supplied the many ships that were using the port. Leith at the time was also well known for its numerous flour mills and sawmills, and also as a major supplier of soap and glass, all helping to increase the prosperity of the town even further. Whale oil was then an important ingredient in the manufacture of soap, and around the end of the 18th century the whalers had started to cast their eye much further afield than local waters for their catch, and were now travelling as far as Greenland and Newfoundland. Much later, led by the Norwegian family Salvesen who had settled in Leith, the whaling industry would expand as far as the Falkland Islands, with its South Georgia harbour named Leith in honour of its Scottish base.

In 1833, the Burgh Reform Act gave Leith the status of parliamentary burgh and therefore independence from Edinburgh. It now had control of its own affairs, including its own Provost, Magistrates, Council, Fire Brigade and Police Force, a situation that would remain in place for 87 years until an unpopular re-amalgamation with Edinburgh in 1920. Then, despite fierce opposition by two former town provosts and its then incumbent John A. Lindsay, an extremely unpopular merger with Edinburgh still went ahead against the wishes of the majority of the townsfolk. An unofficial plebiscite raised by a council worker at the time categorically captured the feeling of most Leithers when 26,810 voted against the merger with only 4,340 voting for it, perhaps giving support to the old adage that if voting changed anything, it would be abolished.

The first few decades of the 20th century saw Leith continue to prosper, particularly during the war years, not only due to its shipbuilding and repair yards, but in all kinds of war-related work. By the 1960s and '70s however, the area had generally been allowed to stagnate into a largely rundown state, with industry in the docks in particular becoming a mere shadow of its earlier dynamic days.

A major redevelopment programme in the 1980s has since seen a total resurgence of the port, particularly around the waterfront. The introduction of the Royal Yacht Britannia was a great boost to the area, as was the construction of both the Ocean Terminal shopping complex and the Scottish Government buildings on the now reclaimed Victoria dock. This, combined with numerous attractive housing developments and an excellent and varied choice of eating places in the town, has allowed Leith once again to recapture the vibrancy and excitement of its earlier days.

At the time of writing, Edinburgh and Leith have managed to cohabitate quite happily for almost a century, but even now anyone born or brought up in the port is still immensely proud of their rich and individual heritage. When asked where they come from, the answer in most cases would invariably still be Leith and not Edinburgh.

The photographs in this book that help paint such a clear and detailed picture of Leith in the late 19th and early 20th century, are from my own private collection. They were gathered together during almost 30 years of trading as Old Scotland in Pictures at 107–109 Brunswick Street in Edinburgh. Some have been seen before, but in no way does this detract from the vibrant story of a historic and unique port.

Dedicated to the men and women
of Leith who fell in both
World Wars and since.

*The children's wing of Leith Hospital which was opened in 1927
as a war memorial for the fallen of the First World War.
Above the entrance, there is an engraving which reads
'LEITH WAR MEMORIAL.
DEDICATED IN MEMORY OF THE MEN
OF LEITH WHO FELL IN
THE GREAT WAR 1914–1918'.*

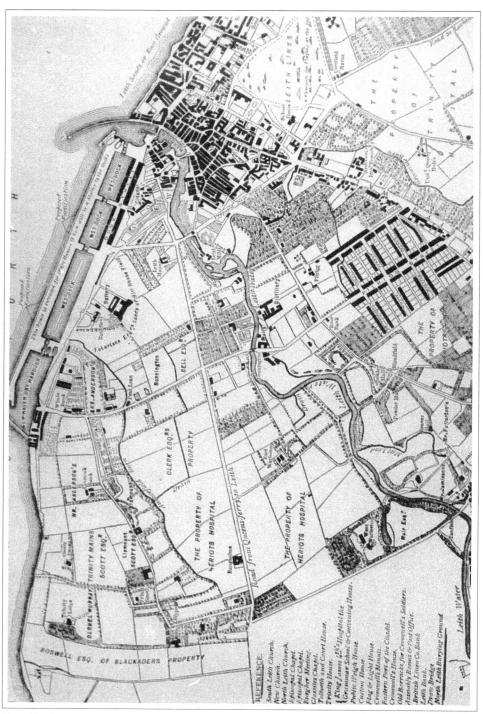

Plan of Leith showing proposed new docks *c.*1804

Plan of Leith c.1883

SECTION I THE FOOT OF THE WALK

For well over 200 years, the **Foot of the Walk**, or 'Fit o' the Walk' as it is more commonly known to the locals, has been recognised as the focal point of the town. It was here that Leithers would gather on a Sunday evening, many known to one another, to discuss the topics of the day. In this photograph taken around the late 1890s, Leith Walk is off to the right, Duke Street is to the left. Marr's Fruiterer and Confectioner shop in the centre has a notice in the window informing customers of a closing down sale. Soon the buildings in the photo would be swept away to make way for the construction of the North British Railway Leith Central Station. Note the beautiful ornate Victorian lamp post on the immediate left of the picture.

View looking along Duke Street (*right*) showing a close-up of the magnificently decorated Victorian lamp post, which once stood at the Foot of the Walk approximately where the statue of Queen Victoria is now situated. The lamp post is no more, a victim of the decision makers of the time in the so-called name of progress. Although it is only a forlorn hope, one wonders if the lamp standard still remains rotting away unrecognised in some corner of a builders yard ready to be reinstalled in some part of the town.

Another view of the Foot of the Walk (*below*) before the demolition to make way for the new station. A meeting appears to be taking place in the centre of the street, which is watched over attentively by a couple of policemen. Originally named Leith Loan, Leith Walk has been the accepted main thoroughfare from the city to the port for well over 200 years. The first main road between Edinburgh and Leith was by way of Restalrig, but by the 17th century the more direct routes of Easter Road, and to a lesser extent Bonnington Road,

had become the more popular. For several hundred years a path had existed along the lines of, what would become in time, Leith Walk, running alongside a defensive ditch and earthen ramparts that had been constructed to defend the town from the threat of Oliver Cromwell in 1650. In time, the rough and uneven earthen rampart would be used by horse-drawn coaches, the roadway later becoming 'a handsome gravel path twenty feet wide, kept in good repair at public expense'. It was only after the opening of the North Bridge, which was designed to link the old town with the rapidly expanding new town, in Edinburgh in 1769 that the more direct Leith Walk route would become the more popular road to the port. Within a few years, Leith Walk would be converted into a proper metalled roadway with a toll house, situated at Shrubhill, to help pay for its upkeep. The tollhouse was demolished in 1834, to be replaced by a custom house.

View looking down Leith Walk c.1900s, taken from the Railway Bridge, which crossed the busy thoroughfare. Jane Street is just off the photo to the left; Manderston Street just off to the right. In 1910, John Gibson, who had offices at 109 Leith Walk, designed and built the first aircraft to be constructed in Scotland in the railway arch at No. 10 Manderson Street; the arch can still be seen. The company failed to prosper, however, even with the burgeoning expansion of flight during the Great War, mainly, it is said, because Government subsidies were granted to larger companies instead. Just a few yards from the railway arches lay the popular Capitol Cinema. Opened on 10 September 1928, the seating capacity of well over 2,000 made the cinema one of the largest establishments in the country. Like many other picture houses it failed to compete with television during the late 1950s and early 1960s, and closed in 1961. The popular Saturday morning Boys and Girls Club transferred to the Regent Cinema at Abbeymount. It later became the first Bingo Hall to be opened in the East of Scotland. The railway bridge crossing Leith Walk was part of the of the Caledonian Railway system that ran between Newhaven and Seafield, crossing by bridge the three main thoroughfares at Bonnington Toll, Leith Walk, and Easter Road. The bridge over the Walk and the one at Bonnington were demolished in the late 1970s and early 1980s, the crossing at Easter Road much earlier.

The completed Leith Walk Station c.1904. The Caledonian

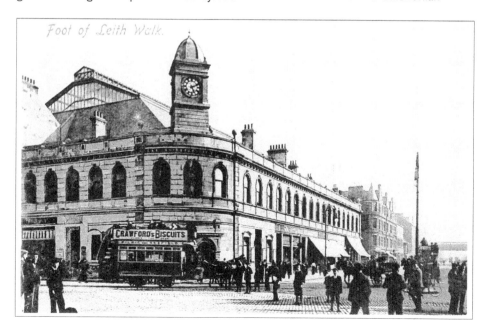

Foot of Leith Walk.

railway bridge which crossed the Walk can be seen in the middle distance. Note the horse-drawn tram in the enter Leith Walk. Horse-drawn trams were first introduced to Leith in January 1874 and were a popular means of transport until the introduction of the electric tram in 1905. The last horse-drawn tram in Edinburgh made its final journey on 21 August 1907. The huge glass-covered roof of the Central Station towers over in the background. The cavernous station interior, while impressive, was in reality far too big for a station comprising of just four platforms, and was perhaps an example of the folly of the North British Railway Company in attempting to compete with the larger, and more successful, Caledonian Railway.

Laying the tram lines for the new electric system at the Foot of the Walk c.1904. (*below*) The Kirkgate is in the middle distance; Kirk Street is on the immediate left.

The Foot of the Walk c.1907. (*below left*) By this time, Leith had switched to the electric tram system which had been introduced in 1905, the new lamp standards supplying the power clearly visible in the middle of the road. The imprint of the famous landmark of Smith and Bowman the Chemists can still be seen on the wall of the middle building adjacent to the Queens Hotel. Both buildings are sandwiched between the Kirkgate on the left and the top of Constitution Street to the right. The hoarding surrounding the soon-to-be-unveiled statue of Queen Victoria is just behind and to the left of the rear tram.

The Foot of the Walk c.1904. Opened on 1 July 1903, the newly completed railway station is on the right hand side of the photograph. Passenger entrances, shops and pubs were to be found at street level on both Leith Walk and Duke Street, the booking office and waiting rooms all situated on the first floor, level with the platforms. A ramp that allowed vehicle access to the station is off to the right of the photo in Crown Place, adjacent to the Tobacco sign on the building. Several tenements at the foot of Easter Road had also been demolished to make way for the construction of the station, which stretched the length of Duke Street, including the centre section of Glover

Street, leaving one section in Duke Street and another in Manderston Street, which was later nicknamed the 'hole in the wall'. When completed, the station was the third largest in the city. A low bridge carrying rail traffic over the foot of Easter Road would also be part of the development. The low level of this bridge, and also the one at Abbeymount, would later cause problems for public transport; a single-decked bus was necessary on the No. 1 circular route. Leith Central Station was constructed by the North British Railway Co mainly to obstruct the expansion in the area by their great competitors, the Caledonian Railway Company, but after a bright start the station failed to capitalise on its early success. It survived a serious fire in the 1930s which severely damaged two of its four platforms without severely curtailing its service, but it closed to passenger travel in 1952. Used thereafter mainly as a depot for diesel engines, the station closed for good in 1972. It was finally demolished in 1999; a supermarket now partly occupies the site.

The Foot of the Walk c.1906.

The electric tram advertising Cadbury's Cocoa is stationary outside the recently-opened Central Station. The building which would later become the Palace Cinema is in the middle distance. The Palace, built on the site of a former wine merchants, was described at the time as a magnificent building erected at enormous cost, believed to be around £20,000, which was a phenomenal sum at that time. It opened its doors on Wednesday 1 January 1913, a few days later than advertised because of industrial problems. It boasted of having electric lighting, but, possibly to reassure patrons who were suspicious of change, it also advertised a gas system as a backup. Beginning its working life as a wine merchants', the building has now almost reverted back to its original use as part of the Wetherspoon's pub chain.

The Foot of the Walk c.1903.
(*top left*) A horse-drawn tram has just left Constitution Street on its way up the Walk. The first horse-drawn tram travelling from Leith to Edinburgh left Bernard Street in 1871, on its way to Haymarket via Constitution Street, Leith Walk and Princes Street. As already mentioned, Leith Walk was originally named Leith Loan. The then-Leith Council decided to ignore the Edinburgh custom of changing street names every hundred yards or so, and the distance between the Foot of the Walk and Pilrig is still simply called Leith Walk to this day. Edinburgh, however, somewhat confusingly, retained the changes every hundred yards or so to incorporate Crichton Place, George Place, Albert Place, Croal Place, Shrubhill Place, Brunswick Place, Elm Row, Haddington Place, Gayfield Place and others.

Trams at the Foot of the Walk outside Central Station c.1911.
(*bottom left*) The No. 200 is yet to be covered while No. 71 on the left has been partly roofed.

Foot of the Walk (*top right*) at the corner of Great Junction Street looking into the Kirkgate, at around the turn of the century. Scott's the Hosier and Hatters warehouse occupies the prominent corner position.

View looking along Great Junction Street (*bottom right*) from the Foot of the Walk, taken just prior to the First World War.

Great Junction Street looking west, c.1900s. (*overleaf, top left*) Constructed along the lines of earlier French fortifications erected to defend the port from the English during the siege of Leith in 1560, the new thoroughfare was designed to link the recently expanded

Leith Docks to the Foot of the Walk. Initially it was named simply Junction Street, but seemingly Junction Road by the locals.

Great Junction Street looking west (*below*) from the Foot of the Walk at around the turn of the century. As can be seen, the area had already become a bustling, thriving thoroughfare. Originally only a rough, uneven track surrounded by very few buildings, Great Junction Street really owes its importance to the growth of North Leith and the new docks. The street was first cobbled in 1868, and the area prospered further with the laying of tram lines that linked the Foot of the Walk with the docks and Newhaven in 1871.

Looking along Junction Street around 1910. (*top right*) The south end of the Kirkgate is on the right, adjacent to Scott's Hat Warehouse. A policeman, complete with sleeping dog at his feet,

keeps a watchful eye on his domain from the safety of the centre island. In the right middle distance bordered by Cables Wynd and Yardheads could be found the home of the famous Crabbies Green Ginger wine. The product had first been invented in Leith as far back as 1801 by John Crabbie, and the company moved to the Great Junction Street premises in the 1850s. Production ended in Leith around 1992, although it is still produced elsewhere in the country. After an absence of several years the company recently re-established contact with Leith, and at the time of writing they are the main sponsors of Hibernian Football Club.

The covered Pilrig-bound tram (*opposite top*) has just left Great Junction Street on its way up Leith Walk past a crowded Foot of the Walk, the scene overseen by the watchful eye of Queen Victoria from her concrete plinth. The attire of most of the crowd suggests that the photo was taken on a Sunday. In the days before family cars, television or Sunday drinking, a stroll on the Links or a chat at the Foot of the Walk was the preferred method of recreation for many Leithers. In such a close-knit community, it it likely that many of the people would have known each other, and the gatherings were a great opportunity to catch up on the local gossip.

Foot of Walk, Leith

The Queen Victoria statue. (*right*)
Situated at the Foot of the Walk
between the Kirkgate and Constitution
Street, the statue was erected in 1907 to
commemorate the Queen's visit to Leith
on 3 September 1842. To the great
disappointment of the town fathers, the
Queen had arrived unexpectedly at
Granton instead of Leith, and a Royal
Arch was hurriedly erected outside Dr
Bell's School in Great Junction Street.
The Queen's imminent arrival created
great excitement in the town, with
crowds lining the streets along the route,
at places four deep, as she passed on her
way to Dalkeith Palace. The plinth also
honours the part played by Territorial
Army soldiers from Leith in the South
African War between 1899–1902. The
statue, which has since been moved a
few feet from its original position, was
sculpted by John Rhind, who would later
carve the Gretna memorial to the Royal
Scots in Rosebank Cemetery.

Junction Road School c.1900s.

(*above*) The school was also known as Doctor Bell's. Bell was responsible for the introduction of the Madras system of education that was copied by many at the time, including several schools in Edinburgh and Newhaven. Born in St Andrews, Dr Bell died in 1838 and is buried in Westminster Abbey. Just off the photograph to the left is Junction Place, also known to the locals as Fire Brigade Street on account of the fire station that had moved there from the Council Chambers in 1877. The station, which changed its name after the merger with Edinburgh on 2 November 1920, would serve the citizens of Leith until the opening of McDonald Road fire station in June 1966. Just opposite the fire station and immediately behind the school is the Leith Swimming Baths, where countless children and adults have learned to swim over the years. Officially opened by councillor Bennet in July 1899, at the time of writing it is still in daily use.

The foot of the Walk and Palace Cinema c.1930.

(*below*) The electric tram on the right is about to exit Duke Street, probably on its way to Edinburgh. With the tram lines of both Leith and the city now unified, the infamous changeover at the 'Pilrig Muddle' was now a thing of the past. Although Edinburgh was noted for its many wide thoroughfares, the tram lines in Duke Street near the Foot of the Walk were 'pinched' to allow tram cars to traverse the narrow street at this point, just one of several similar single-line arrangements in the city. The apparel of some of the youngsters in the photograph suggests that they were about to, or had, taken part, in an event; possibly the Leith Hospital pageant or some other festival on Leith Links.

SECTION 2 THE KIRKGATE

The top of the Kirkgate c.1909. (*above*) Trinity House on the left of the photograph and the wall of South Leith Church on the right are the only buildings to survive demolition in the 1960s. Founded in the 14th century as a hospital for seafarers, the present Trinity House was built on the site of a later 1816 building. Two stones, dated 1555 and 1570, can be found on a side wall. Now a maritime museum, Trinity House contains a magnificent collection of artefacts commemorating Leith's historical connection with the sea, including a magnificent stained glass window which was commissioned in 1933 as a tribute to all who had served in the Merchant Navy throughout the years, and is well worth a visit.

The Kirkgate (*right*) around the turn of the century. The much acclaimed Gaiety Theatre is on the right of the photograph,

also the entrance to the pit Gallery. The building, originally a church, was opened as a theatre in 1886, but had a very short existence, for it burned down two years later. It reopened the following year as the New Princes Theatre, and it was renamed the New Gaiety in 1899. Now featuring electric light, it was also said to be the only theatre in the city at that time to hold an alcohol licence. Originally a music hall and theatre, it converted to a cinema just prior to the First World War. In 1944 variety returned when Will Fyffe

performed the official opening. Throughout the years many illustrious performers have appeared at the theatre including the world famous escapologist, Harry Houdini, who performed on stage between June and July 1905, and latterly Leith's own popular variety star Johnny Victory. The Scottish comedian Johnny Beattie and the Four Kordites were the last performers to appear at the theatre before it finally closed its doors for the last time in 1956. The building was demolished along with the rest of the Kirkgate in the early '60s.

Giles Street (*below*) showing the probably well-used Kate McGourty's pawn shop and furniture store. Giles Street was but one of a warren of narrow streets and closes that bordered the Kirkgate. The inferior and overcrowded housing, particularly in Giles Street and nearby Coalhill, posed a significant danger to health, and much of the area was later swept away after the passing of the Leith Improvement Scheme in 1885. It is said that at that time the infant mortality rate could be as high as 55 per cent, with many brought into this world amidst squalor and run-down surroundings.

The Kirkgate. (*opposite top*) Often described as the heart of Leith, the photograph was taken shortly before its demolition in the 1960s. The famous policeman, Willie Merrilees, who would later rise to the rank of Chief Constable, was born in a top floor flat in St Andrews Street, just off the Kirkgate. The well-known Leith Victoria Boxing Club, founded by Robb's shipyard workers and other boxing enthusiasts in 1919, and thought to be the second oldest surviving boxing club in Britain, had clubrooms in the street. The famous Lonsdale Belt winner Tancy Lee would later become an instructor. Born in Leith in 1882, Lee swept through the amateur ranks and won the British Flyweight championship, becoming the first Scotsman to win a Longsdale belt when defeating the Welsh

boxer Jimmy Wilde at the National Sporting Club in London on 25 January 1915; the referee stopped the fight in the 17th round. Lee would later train the exciting Edinburgh boxer Johnny Hill, who was born in Brunswick Road. Hill became Scotland's first ever World Champion boxer when he defeated the American 'Newsboy' Brown at Clapton Orients football ground in August 1928, aged 23. Tragically, only a few months later, he complained of feeling unwell while training. Diagnosed as suffering from pneumonia, he died soon after. Lee himself would die in 1941. Much later, Leith-born George Smith would become the first Scotsman to referee a professional World Heavyweight Championship fight when he took charge of the Henry Cooper versus Muhammad Ali contest at Highbury Stadium in London in 1966. Like Smith, another personality closely associated with the club was Eugene Henderson who refereed several World Championship

fights including the famous World Middleweight bout between Randolph Turpin and Sugar Ray Robinson in London in 1951. The fight, which saw Turpin defeat the reigning champion, is still reckoned by many to have been the greatest title fight seen in this country.

The Kirkgate has yet another claim to fame. It is said that in 1841 Charles Drummond, a printer from Leith, sold the country's first ever Christmas card from his premises on the street.

The Kirkgate (*below*) just prior to demolition in the 1960s.

The Kirkgate (*above*) just prior to demolition in the 1960s.

The foot of the Kirkgate looking towards Tolbooth Wynd, just prior to the area being bulldozed in the early 1960s. The corner of Water Street and Charlotte (now Queen Charlotte) Street is in the middle distance. The buildings in Water Street replaced earlier housing that had been demolished just before the First World War. Water Street, once called Water Lane, took its name from a reservoir, or 'pipes', which had at one time been situated near the foot of the Kirkgate.

Tolbooth Wynd looking towards Henderson Street c.1904. (*above*) The Kirkgate is just off the photograph to the left. At that time a camera would be relatively rare and the novelty was sure to attract an inquisitive crowd in great numbers, many of the children in bare feet. In the early days the Tolbooth Wynd was considered a very important thoroughfare, second only to the Kirkgate. The Cinema House, which opened in 1913 and showed newfangled moving pictures, was situated on the corner of the Wynd and Henderson Street.

Tolbooth Wynd c.1900s. (*right*) The future premises of Manclark's, at the bottom end of the Kirkgate, is in the distance. Around the 16th century, the original signal tower was built near this spot, its function later becoming obsolete with the creation of buildings between the street and the sea. The Signal Tower at the Shore, built in 1685 as a windmill,

eventually took over the purpose after its conversion from a rapeseed mill. Tolbooth Wynd took its name from a Tolbooth, or prison, which was built nearby in 1565. Even with what would probably have been a grim and foreboding edifice in the area, the Wynd, one of the roads that led to the bridge over the river, was still described at the time as being an extremely picturesque approach to the harbour.

SECTION 3 THE SHORE

An early engraving of the pier at the shore, (*above*) taken from Grant's *Old and New Edinburgh* c.1880s. Before the reclamation of the land to build the Edinburgh and Imperial docks, the sea would almost lap the base of the Signal Tower at the Shore. Behind the buildings on the right lay the famous Leith Sands. It was here that the popular historical Leith Race Week took place, an event regularly attended by the King. With a two mile course stretching to Seafield and back, the race days were always keenly anticipated by the townsfolk, the busy carnival atmosphere enhanced by the many stalls, booths and drinking areas, both on the sands itself and in the town. During the early part of the 17th century, however, the increased level of drunkenness and rowdiness associated with the event led to the more popular races being transferred to Musselburgh. Minor horse racing continued until the

reclamation of the area from the sea for the construction of the new docks in the 19th century.

An early view of the drawbridges at the Shore c.1880s. (*below*) Bernard Street bridge and the corner of Commercial Street are in the middle distance. There is now no trace of the drawbridge at the front of the photograph that was built to enable train traffic to cross the harbour to the then-new East and West Wet Docks from a

spot near the entrance to Timber bush on the Shore. This bridge was probably demolished at the same time as the Bernard Street drawbridge in 1897. The masts of ships in the inner harbour can be seen in the distance.

The Sailors' Home and Signal Tower (*top*) on the Shore around the turn of the century. On the right of the Tower is the Albert Engine Works, premises of John Cran and Company Shipbuilders. Cran's was one of the leading shipbuilders in the area, who would later merge to become Cran and Sommerville. Starting operation in Leith in the mid 1880s, the company only ceased to trade in the years leading up to the Second World War. The photograph clearly shows the perennial problem of the low level of water in the harbour at low tide, serious enough to cause severe disruption to shipping and consequently a loss of trade. In all likelihood, the paddle steamer in the foreground is beached on

the sand, helpless until high water allowed movement.

The new swing bridge at Bernard Street (*above*) looking towards Commercial Street and Customs House at the turn of the century. Except for a new concrete bridge over the river in the 1960s and the absence of traffic, the scene remains almost the same today.

View of the harbour around the turn of the century (*overleaf top*) taken from the arched entrance to Timber Bush. Work is taking place on

a ship in Menzies' graving dock on the right. The opening on the left, behind the rear of the Custom House, is the entrance to the East and West wet Docks.

View of the Sailors' Home and Signal Tower from the opposite shore c.1894. (*below*) The large ship is probably about to enter the wet Docks. The old salt sitting on the capstan has obviously been superimposed, possibly to enhance a view that would later be used on a postcard.

The inner harbour and Shore looking north in the late 1890s. (*above*) In the middle background the Bernard Street Drawbridge can be seen in the raised position. The drawbridge was demolished in 1897 to be replaced by a swing bridge which in itself made way for the present permanent structure in the 1960s. Most of the buildings on the right have also long been swept away, the site occupied for a time by the Leith Labour Exchange and now a restaurant. The Sandport Street drawbridge is just out of the picture on the left.

A busy outer harbour c.1900s

The Sailors' Home c.1912.
Replacing an earlier mission in Dock Place, the Sailors' Home opened 29 January 1881 at a cost of over £9,000. It was described at the time as the most complete establishment of its kind in the country. Over the years the building has been a welcome refuge for thousands of sailors visiting the port, including many that had been shipwrecked. Later known as the Angel, the building would lie in a derelict state for several years, before

reverting to a hotel in 1994. It is now home to branch of the Malmaison Hotel chain in an area that has become upmarket in recent years.

The Sailors' Home and Signal Tower taken from the opposite shore c.1900s. (*above*) The buildings are immediately opposite what was once the entrance to the old East and West docks. The tower was originally built as a mill, one of three in Leith. At one time the tower was capped by a wooden structure; this was removed and castellated battlements were added during the Napoleonic Wars and its use changed to a signal tower to relay information to shipping about the depth

of water in the harbour. The ship alongside Crans Albert Engine Works is the Britannia sailing from Leith.

View of the Sailors' Home and Tower from Customs House. (*below left*) The ship on the right hand side of the picture, in front of the Albert Engine works of John Cran, is again the *Britannia*. Over a century later the port would be reunited with a ship of that name when the Royal Yacht *Britannia* berthed permanently as a floating museum only a few hundred yards away on 11 October 1998.

The outer harbour and shore at the turn of the century. (*right*) The corner of Bernard Street and Kings Wark are in the right middle distance. Four of the ships that would be involved in the disastrous Darrien Scheme left from Leith Roads on 26 July 1698, hoping to set up a colony in South America and open up new trade routes. The ships contained 1,200 settlers and over 300 crew. The following year several other

ships sailed from the Clyde to join them, but the scheme was an unmitigated disaster, due in no small way to opposition from the powerful East India Company. The remains of the expedition returned the following year after losing one ship, yet another seriously damaged, and only half of the men, with the majority of the others dying of fever. The over-ambitious scheme almost bankrupted the country and would lead directly to a union with England in 1707.

The Shore c.1930s. (*below*) The ship is moored alongside the spot where King George IV landed in 1822, the historic event now marked with a plaque. The

outline of the Victoria Swing Bridge can be seen on the left. In memory of a bygone age, what appears to be a cast iron gents urinal can be seen level with the ship's bow. It was at this very spot that a famous incident took place in 1779, which was to end in tragic consequences. In April that year, highlanders from the 42nd and 71st regiments were sent to Leith for embarkation to Egypt. On arriving at the Shore, rumours quickly spread that the soldiers were to be ordered to wear trews instead of the traditional kilt and they refused to board the ship lying in the outer harbour. A large detachment of troops was sent from Edinburgh to escort the mutineers back to the castle if they still disobeyed orders to board. Tragically the situation quickly got out of hand when a sergeant attempted to restrain a mutineer who tried to escape. The sergeant was run through by one of the mutineers, and all hell broke loose. Shots were fired by both sides, and by the time order was restored 14 soldiers from both sides had been killed, including the captain sent from the castle, and over 20 wounded.

Today, the 400 ton former Royal Naval minesweeper 'Samuel Green' is permanently moored at the location. Built in Greenock just after the First World War, and once owned by the Guinness family, it was saved from the breakers' yard in the early 1980s by an entrepreneur who brought the vessel to Leith to be used as a floating restaurant renamed the 'Ocean Mist'. Despite changing hands several times throughout the years, the ship was in a seriously derelict state, until refurbished by new owners and converted back into a bar/ restaurant.

The King's Wark at the turn of the century. (*below*) The present building replaced an earlier structure of that name, which had been erected by King James I on the site in 1434. The building, consisting of accommodation, warehouses, shops and pubs, was burned to the ground in 1554 by the Earl of Hereford's men when they swept through the port after landing at Granton. Later rebuilt, a tennis court belonging to the property was converted into a weigh house in 1649. The present building, one of the oldest in Leith, and once popularly known as the 'Jungle', received major restoration work in the 1970s and is now a restaurant.

The Shore from Sandport Bridge. (*bottom*) The opening to Burgess Street is on the left. All the main buildings in the photo have been swept away to be replaced by modern houses and commercial properties. It is said that the

in 1493, a stone bridge built here in 1787. Using the original foundations, this was later converted to a drawbridge, which allowed larger craft access to the numerous shipbuilding and ship repairing yards that then lined both sides of the river.

The Shore c.1912 showing the corner of Bernard Street on the left. (*left*) The Kings Wark is the large white-painted building on the opposite corner. The river is clearly at low tide. With the construction of new lock gates at the harbour mouth in the late 1960s, both the docks and harbour are now non-tidal.

A similar view of the Shore (*left*) taken from an old postcard around the same time.

first bridge to cross the Water of Leith at the shore was built about a hundred yards upriver from the present Sandport Bridge

Sailing boats in the inner harbour at the turn of the last century. Sandport Bridge is just out of the picture

on the left. The recently opened swing bridge crossing from Bernard Street to Commercial Street is in the distance.

The Shore and inner harbour from the junction of Coalhill and Henderson Street c.1906. (*below*) Again, the recently completed Swing Bridge at Bernard Street can be seen in middle distance. The depth of the water, particularly in the inner harbour, was a constant problem that restricted the size of shipping in the river, as can be seen by the relatively small dimensions of the craft in the photograph, and consequently the size of vessels that could be constructed or repaired in the several shipyards that inhabited the area. The bonded warehouse in the background that fronts on to Commercial Street has now been converted into modern flats.

The Shore c.1905. (*above*) Although the people going about their day-to-day business seem completely unaware of the

presence of the camera, it would appear that the ever-vigilant Leith 'copper' in the middle of the road is alive to the situation.

Bernard Street, Swing Bridge and river c.1922. (*overleaf top left*) Taken from the building at the corner of Commercial Street, the Swing Bridge and its workings can clearly be seen. Also note the metal connection arches on the bridge that carried power for the electric trams. The current for the trams would be broken when the bridge was open; the contact breakers on the metal arches allowed the power supply to be

reconnected when the bridge closed. Considering the continuous problem regarding the depth of water in the harbour it is perhaps surprising to see a ship of its size at this point.

A closed-roof tram crossing Bernard Street Bridge, perhaps on its way to Granton via Newhaven c.1928. (*above*) Taken from the inner harbour.

The Shore and inner harbour looking south, taken between the Wars. (*top right*) The corner of Burgess Street and the opening of Henderson Street are on the left; the closed arms of the Sandport Street Swing Bridge is in the middle distance. The Paddle Steamer on the right alongside the bonded warehouse helps create an idyllic image.

An unusual view of the Shore and east side of Custom House taken from adjacent rooftops probably around the 1950s, (*above*) giving a

good view of the Bernard Street bridge and its swing apparatus. Again, the size of the ship in the photograph is perhaps surprising given the relative shallowness of the water at this point.

Poor quality view of the Sandport drawbridge and Coalhill c.1950s, (*below*) taken from the top of a building at the corner of Commercial Street. As already mentioned, the first stone bridge to cross the river in Leith was built at this spot during the late 16th and early 17th centuries, but the later construction of a swing bridge in the 1800s allowed larger

ships access to the many shipyards that lined both sides of the river.

Alexander Walker's horse and cart making its way along the Shore at the inner harbour, possibly around the 1950s. (*below*) The bonded warehouses on the far side of the river are in the background alongside one of the several graving docks that once populated the area. Walker was only one of the many carters who had once been a familiar sight in the area before the total domination of the motor vehicle, and it is sometimes difficult to remember that horse and carts could still be seen on the streets of the town as recently as the 1960s.

Lamb's House c.1920s. (*right*)
Lamb's House is thought by some to be the original house of the prominent Leith businessman, Andrew Lamb, in which Mary Queen of Scots is said to have spent a short period of time after her arrival in Leith in 1561. However, it is almost certain that the present building is of a much later date, although probably built on the site of the original. By the beginning of the 1900s the house had been subdivided into eight rented flats, but by the 1930s the house had fallen

into disrepair. Restored at a considerable cost just prior to the Second World War, the building came under the care of the National Trust for Scotland in 1958. In 1962 the Queen Mother officially opened the converted premises as a day centre for retired people, the first such venture in the country.

A decrepit looking Lamb's House in the early 1950s (*below*) now empty and boarded up. The warehouses in Water Street, which have now been converted into private flats as part of the recent regeneration of Leith, are on the right.

Coalhill, site of Mary of Guise House (demolished 1887). (*right*) Mary of Guise, who was married to King James V, was the mother of Mary Queen of Scots, and Queen Regent of Scotland. She is believed to have lived in a house on this spot, although this is disputed by many historians. She died in Edinburgh Castle, where she had sought refuge at the height of the reformation, and her body was transported back to France. Her death is said to have signalled the end of the French garrison in the port, although French influence remained in the area for a considerable time. Coalhill was the site of the original Council Chambers, but by the middle 1800s both it and the neighbouring Giles Street were described as being particularly unpleasant

places in which to live. Designated a slum area in 1877, both Coalhill and the adjacent Giles Street would soon be demolished.

Another view of the site of the Mary of Guise House. (*above*) The small stone structure on the right is possibly one of the five wells that were situated around the town to supply fresh water to the locals, one said to have been located near this spot.

Sir John Gladstone, father of the future Prime Minister William Ewart Gladstone, was born in Leith on 11 December 1864. Sir John was a successful businessman and later an MP, and the family is said to have had premises in Coalhill. Although born in England, William Gladstone remained proud of his Scottish roots. He served four different spells as Prime Minister between 1868 and 1894, more than any other politician. His father, Sir John, is buried in North Leith burial ground.

A bit of old Leith. (*top right*) A poor quality photograph possibly showing Sheriff Brae looking north towards Coalhill and the Shore c.1900s. According to legend, the name Coalhill had nothing to do with coal but took its name from an area where the game of Quoits was played.

Henderson Street c.1950s. (*above*) The one-way street sign on the left points towards the east side of Giles Street, which crossed Henderson Street at this point. The fondly-remembered Broad Pavement is on the right, a playground to many generations of Leith children. The site of the Broad Pavement, and the adjacent Corporation buildings that lay just behind, is now occupied by the 'Banana Flats' that were constructed in the late 1960s. The vaults in Giles Street, once used to store the vast amounts of wine that was imported into Leith from France, are still used to this day by the Scotch Malt Whisky Society.

Bridge Street from Sandport Bridge c.1960s. (*overleaf top left*) The opening to Dock Street is in the right middle distance. The buildings in the photograph, including a branch of the Leith Provident grocery store, or the 'Provie', would soon be demolished.

Another view of Bridge Street probably taken on the same day. (*above*) What appears to be a lorry belonging to the British Road Services can be seen making its way towards Sandport Bridge and presumably its depot in Seafield Road.

Couper Street is situated just off Coburg Street (*below*) Couper Street is situated just off Coburg Street opposite North Leith burial ground and was for many years home to the well-known Melrose's Tea Warehouse. The school opened in 1890 and closed on 29 June 1951. It was later used for a short while as a college for mechanical and engineering apprentices from Ferranti's. Both the school and most of the buildings in Couper Street were demolished in the 1970s. The street may well have a military claim to fame. It is believed that Sapper Adam Archibald may have been born in number 49 on 14 January 1879, although this is disputed by some who think he may have been born at 40 Balfour Street, just off Leith Walk. During the closing days of the Great War in November 1918, Archibald, then aged 29, became one of only two Leithers to win the Victoria Cross in the First World War, when he showed gallantry above and beyond the call of duty by continuing to attempt to erect a

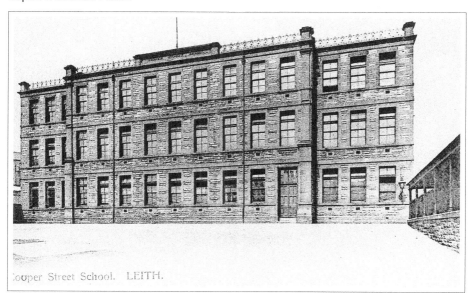

Couper Street School. LEITH.

temporary bridge over a river under extreme enemy fire. During this attempt, he collapsed due to the effects of gas poisoning. He died in Leith in 1957, aged 78. His VC is on display at the Royal Engineers Museum at Chatham in Kent.

Another VC winner was born only a hundred yards or so from Couper Street, at 2 Maderia Place in 1880, and it is possible in such a close knit community that the two may well have known each other. At Missy in France on 14 September 1914, Captain William Johnston of the Royal Engineers continually supplied ammunition by barge over a river, returning several times with wounded colleagues while under heavy fire. Unfortunately, he was killed at Ypres on 8 June 1915. Like Archibald, Johnston's VC is also on display at the Royal Engineers Museum at Chatham.

There is one other winner of the Victoria Cross who may be considered to come under the Leith banner, although he was born in Trinity on 5 March 1883. On 21 March 1918, Lieutenant Allan Ker of the Gordon Highlanders won the Victoria Cross near San Quentin for conspicuous gallantry in the face of the enemy. Faced with overwhelming odds he refused to leave his wounded men and continued to repel several German attacks for over three hours until forced to surrender. Later promoted to Major, he survived the closing stages of the War and died in London on 12 September 1958. In 1991 his Victoria Cross was sold to a private buyer for £15,500.

The Customs House and Commercial Street c.1900s.
The Custom House was opened in 1812 at a cost of £12,617. Built on the site of the Sandport, which was constructed in 1780 and reputed to be the first dry dock in Leith, the ornate stepped frontage of the Custom House was added at a later date. On the evening of 4 February 1881, police received reports that several

people had been accosted by two armed men in the vicinity of Ferry Road. Shortly after, police officers observed two men acting suspiciously outside the Customs House. When asked to accompany the officers to the police station, the men drew their guns, shooting the policemen, wounding both. Hotly pursued by reinforcements, who had arrived at the scene, they shot another officer in the leg. Before he could be apprehended, one of the desperadoes put the gun to his head and shot himself dead. His companion was soon captured a short distance away near Admiralty Street, but only after his pistol had misfired several times as he attempted to shoot his pursuer. The man later received 14 years of hard labour. The two ruffians were later described as members of the infamous Ned Kelly gang who had arrived in the country from Australia only a few days before. Later, all six constables who had joined the chase received a medal and a cash reward for their part in the affray.

Commercial Street looking east c.1920s. The Customs House on is on the left. The opening to Sandport Street, identified by the ray of sunlight between the buildings, is on the right. A short distance to the west, behind the camera, once lay the Citadel. After the Battle of Dunbar in September 1650, Cromwell's troops occupied Edinburgh and Leith. It was decided to erect five forts throughout Scotland, and under the command of General Monck a Citadel was built at Leith to defend the town and harbour. Constructed in the shape of a pentagon on ground previously partly occupied by the burial grounds of North Leith Church, its walls ran roughly several hundred yards along what is now Commercial Street before turning east into Dock Street. Turning south to follow the approximate line of the present Coburg Street, it turned right again near Couper Street, with yet another turn to rejoin Commercial Street. Occupying several acres of land and erected at a

cost of over £100,000, which was mainly raised under duress by the people of Leith, the fort was not a success and after the restoration of the royalty in 1661 it was ordered to be demolished; all except for the north walls, which created a barrier to the sea. Parts of the old Citadel were used for different purposes throughout the years, including for a short while a prison, but by 1779 little remained of the fortifications. What was left was finally demolished shortly after the Second World War, and the land was used for commercial development. Before the area was reclaimed to build the wet docks at the start of the 19th century most of what would later become Commercial Street lay under the waters of the Forth, and it is said that in 1800 the bowsprit of a ship that had been driven aground in a severe gale could be heard beating itself against the walls of the Citadel, before the ship was broken into pieces by the waves. Only the original, main, or east, entrance to the fortifications at Dock Street remains. In later years, flats were built on the top of this substantial arched gateway, but, like the Citadel itself, these have also been consigned to history.

Dock Place c.1920. The original gateway to the wet docks, the first to be built in the port, is on the left of the photo just behind the warehouses. Both docks were later surrounded on the Commercial Street side by Bonds and other warehouses. Both docks have now been filled in: the site is now partly occupied by the Scottish Office and the Bonded warehouses have been converted into flats. Now all that remains of the original East and West docks, apart from the gateway, is the original narrow channel on the north of Dock Place, which once served as the connection between the docks and the inner harbour on the Shore.

SECTION 4 THE DOCKS

On 22 September 1896, Nicholas II, the last Czar of Russia, the Czarina and their baby daughter Princes Olga visited Leith. As the Imperial Yacht *Standart* lay off Leith Roads, the Royal couple received a thunderous gun salute from the Channel Fleet, which had arrived in the River Forth specifically for the occasion. Wearing the ceremonial uniform of the Royal Scots Greys, for which he was Honorary Colonel-in-Chief, Nicholas and his esteemed party, including the Prince of Wales, boarded the paddle steamer 'Tantallon Castle' for the short journey to Victoria Quay. Here, they they were received by Provost Bennet of Leith, Lord Provost McDonald of Edinburgh and other distinguished guests. After a short ceremony the royal couple made their way towards Junction Street Station, where they would travel by train to meet Queen Victoria at Balmoral. All along the flag-festooned streets the royal couple were received by enthusiastic crowds, whose excitement was not lessened by the torrential rain. Nicholas was the first Russian ruler to visit Scotland, although his father, Nicholas I, had visited England in 1884. On the night of 16–17 July 1918, Nicholas II and his entire family would meet their deaths at the hands of the Bolsheviks.

View of the Edinburgh Dock during the early days of the new century. (*overleaf*) The pump house, now a listed building, is in the middle distance. The U-shaped Edinburgh docks were opened in 1881 by the Duke of Edinburgh. They were the first such undertaking since the building of the Albert Dock 16 years before.

Grain Elevator at the Edinburgh Dock c.1930s. (*right*) Throughout the years the main import into Leith had been grain. Regular supplies were received, mostly from North America, but also from Russia. Malting barley came from America, Syria and North Africa, and the busy trade helped to provide the large workforce with regular employment. To cope with the increase in demand a huge grain elevator was built at the Seafield end of the Edinburgh dock and another at the north side of the Albert dock.

Leith Docks c.1900s. (*overleaf top*) The invention of steam power allowed the building of much larger ships, and by the end of the 18th century both the inner and outer harbours on the shore were unable to cope with the increased demand on the port. Made with stone transported by sea from a quarry near Rosyth Castle in Fife, the East Dock became the first purpose built dock in Leith with an entrance out into the outer harbour in 1806. The adjacent West dock followed in 1817, complete with two graving docks. Plans to add another dock to link up with the deeper water at Newhaven in the west were abandoned because of the cost. The sandbank that

surrounded Leith for about half a mile into the Forth had long been a source of irritation, making the movement of shipping into Leith at all states of the tide both inconvenient and dangerous. In 1851 the harbour had been deepened with the extension of the East Pier and the construction of a new West Pier, but even this improvement gave only an extra few feet of draft. During the next 50 years or so, over 80 acres of shoreline stretching from the mouth of the river as far as Seafield, including the famous Leith sands, would be reclaimed to make way for much-needed expansion. The Edinburgh Docks were opened in 1881 and the Imperial Dock in 1902.

An extremely congested Leith docks in the 1880s. (*right*) The ships often lined up three, or sometimes four abreast, which illustrates just how busy the port could be and outlines the need for further expansion. A report to the treasury in 1846 pointed out that the docks were now severely

overcrowded, that there was a lack of a graving dock to accommodate the ever larger ships, that there was an absence of a low water jetty for passengers and light haulage, and that at low tide the harbour was all but dry. Particular mention was also made regarding the large amount of rubbish that was regularly washed downriver to end up in the harbour, and the obvious hazard it posed to health. In an attempt to alleviate the overcrowding problem, the Victoria Dock, the first to be constructed since the opening of the West Dock in 1817, was opened in 1852. Somewhat appropriately, it was officially opened to the accompaniment of great celebration when the steamship Royal Victoria became the first ship to enter the new dock.

The Albert and Imperial docks c.1920s. (*below*) Opened in 1902, the Imperial Dock (in the background) was the last to be built in Leith. A ship can be seen in one of the two small engraving docks that led off the Albert Dock. Several of the many derricks and coal hoists that could be found in the area dominate the background. The Albert Dock, costing almost £300,000 to construct, was opened on 21 August 1869, when the SS *Florence* broke the ribbon to become the first ship to enter the new dock.

The grain elevator between the Imperial and Albert docks c.1930s. (*left*)

A pleasure steamer leaving the docks c.1900s. (*right*) Victoria Swing Bridge, completed in 1874 and at the time the largest in the country, is in the background. Victoria Quay, the landing place of Russian Czar Nicholas II in 1896, is on the right. What would soon

become Robb's Shipyard is just out of the picture, also on the right. The ship in the foreground is just one of the many pleasure craft plying their trade from the Forth at that time. These were extremely popular with passengers and regular trips were made from Leith, Newhaven and Granton to destinations at Aberdour, Pettycur Bay, Burntisland, Stirling and the recently-opened Forth Railway Bridge.

Another view of the inner harbour around 1904 (*below*) showing one of the many paddle steamers that plied their trade from Leith, possibly the same 'Tantallon Castle' which had carried Czar Nicholas II to Leith in 1896. Once again, Victoria Bridge can be seen in the background with the Sailors' Home also easily identified by its huge clock face. On the left of the picture, a tall sailing ship is about to enter the recently-opened Imperial Dock.

King George VI and Queen Elizabeth during their wartime visit to Robb's shipyard in 1943. Robb's was first established in 1918. After acquiring several other small yards in the area during the 1920s, the company became known as the Victoria Shipyard. With the country then at war with Germany, King George and Queen Elizabeth visited the yard on 29 July 1943. At that time, the tide had turned for the Allies, with Robb's playing a major part in events. During the First World War only two small ships had been built in Leith, but in the second global conflict, Robb's had constructed 42 ships for the Admiralty, mostly frigates and corvettes, and another 12 for the Merchant Navy. In addition, between the years 1939 and 1945 an incredible 2807 ships, both Merchant and Royal Navy, had been repaired. This was an average of more than one a day, and included on a couple of occasions the destroyer HMS *Cossack*. In February 1940 the crew of the *Cossack* had risen to fame for boarding the German ship *Altmark* in the Norwegian Jossingfiord to rescue captured British sailors with the now famous cry, 'The Navy's here', despite a neutral Norwegian patrol boat insisting that the *Altmark* had already been inspected. The prisoners had earlier been transferred from the German pocket battleship *Admiral Graf Spee*, which had been scuttled after the Battle of the River Plate in December 1939. The 229 freed merchantmen were brought into Leith to a rapturous welcome from the locals. Unfortunately the *Cossack* was sunk by U-568 in October the following year.

Robb's had also played a prominent part in the D-Day invasion by constructing several sections of the ingenious

Mulberry Harbour and pontoons, which were destined to play such a major role in the final victory. By amazing coincidence, several of the Leith-built sections had been towed to Normandy by the rescue tugs HMS *Growler* and HMS *Samsonia*, which were both built in the yard.

After the War the company returned once more to peacetime activity, and in 1977 they purchased the Caledon Shipbuilding Company of Dundee to become known as Robb Caledon Shipbuilding. However, like most of the shipyards in the country, the company found orders hard to come by and closed its doors for the last time in 1983, bringing to an end more than 500 years of shipbuilding in Leith. The site is now occupied by the Ocean Terminal shopping complex. The area, however, still retains a link with royalty with the acquisition of the former Royal Yacht *Britannia* as a tourist attraction in the late 1990s

The King and Queen inspecting the yard on their morale boosting trip to Robb's in the summer of 1943, watched by an appreciative workforce.

The East and West Piers from an old engraving c.1880s. As already mentioned, the low level of water caused by the sandbank that stretched over half a mile into the Forth at the mouth of the harbour, particularly at low tide, had been a constant source of concern for years, and regularly resulted in either a loss of, or disruption to, trade.

Now, with the advent of steam, which allowed the construction of much larger ships, the problem had been exacerbated. This was a situation which was of great advantage to the new deep water piers at Newhaven and Granton, and with the loss of revenue something had to be done. During the 1770s the harbour had been widened and dredged and the stone pier extended by almost 100 yards, but these measures had only increased the depth of water by a few feet. On 15 August 1826, work started on extending the original pier by a further 500 yards. The project took two years to complete, and, in 1876, the foundation stone was laid for the construction of an extension to the West Pier which would be strong enough to take a rail line. When it was completed in 1878, it stretched over 500 yards into the river. Both new piers had cost over £45,000 to complete, an astronomical sum at that time, but it did not completely eradicate the problem: the depth of water once again increased by only a few feet, and the area between the piers and the inner harbour still required almost constant dredging. It was a problem which would not be eradicated until the completion of new dock gates in the 1960s.

Passengers boarding an excursion steamer at the West Pier c.1890s. (*below*) In the 19th century pleasure trips had increased in popularity and there were regular sailings from Leith and Newhaven to destinations in Fife and as far as Stirling. Trips to see the construction of the Forth Railway Bridge at Queensferry had also become increasingly popular, particularly after its completion in 1890. In Leith the competition was fierce, and several companies competed for trade, including the well-known firm Galloway's.

An excursion steamer leaving the West Pier c.1900s. (*top right*) The paddle steamer in the background is empty, possibly awaiting the next consignment of passengers. The harbour mouth can be seen in the middle distance.

A sailing ship leaving the docks past the East Pier (*below*) under the control of the pilot boat. Another ship lies waiting in the background ready to enter the dock.

The West Pier. (*bottom left*) A pleasure steamer has just entered the harbour ready to moor at the quay. The signal

apparatus at the extreme end of the pier informed incoming vessels of the depth of water in the harbour at the time. In the early days of the 19th century a fever isolation hospital was said to have been situated near the end of the pier. One can only begin to imagine the terror of the, in some cases already seriously ill, patients, who were subjected to the severe storms that regularly swept the area in such a precarious and isolated position over half a mile from the safety of the shore. In December 1871, fire broke out on the pier when workmen coating the exposed wooden pillars with preservative accidentally set fire to the melted pitch, resulting in a large section in the middle of the pier being completely destroyed, and leaving only 300 yards at the shore end and 100 yards at the outer end intact.

View of old East and West docks looking west c.1920s. (*overleaf*) Both docks have now been completely filled in, and the area now abounds with quality restaurants and pubs. The bonded warehouses on the left have been

converted into flats. In the middle distance the Training Ship Dolphin, which was attached to the nearby Nautical College, can be seen with its distinctive black and white livery. The graving dock in the right foreground and the warehouses have also completely disappeared, and the site is now partly occupied by the Scottish Office. The three-masted barque Dolphin had a chequered history. Built at Middlesbrough and launched in December 1882, the ship saw action against the Sudanese Chief Osman Dinga in the defence of Suakin, and was reputed to have been the first ship to use the only recently invented searchlight in battle. Refitted after the end of the First World War, using metal from the recently decommissioned battleship King George V, she later became a submarine supply ship. Following decommission, it was purchased with a view to converting it into a floating museum. While on tow to Scotland the ship took on water as she approached the River Forth and was

beached near Fisherrow. After repairs she was towed to a berth in the West Old Harbour at Leith in 1928, where she remained until moving briefly to the East Harbour, when the West Harbour was filled in in 1965, and then later the Inner Harbour, before finally being broken up at Bo'ness in 1969. During her time in Leith the Dolphin became first a boys' club, and in 1944 a boys' training ship. She suffered minor damage during the Second World War when debris from a German bomb, which fell on nearby Constitution Street near the foot of Portland Place, landed on her deck.

The yard in the right foreground was the premises of Menzies and Company Shipbuilders. The Paddle Steamer Sirius, which became the first steamship to cross the Atlantic from east to west in April 1838, was built at the yard. The Sirius beat off the challenge of Isambard Kingdom Brunel's Great Western, whose attempt at the record was delayed by a serious fire, arriving in America a few days later. On the trip over the Atlantic, the Sirius ran out of fuel, only managing to complete the journey by burning anything on board which was flammable. Unfortunately the Sirius was lost in January 1847 with heavy loss of life when she foundered on rocks off Bally Cotton Bay in Ireland during a heavy fog. The narrow channel on the left of the photograph is all that remains today of the original entrance to the Old East and West docks.

HMS *Claverhouse* moored in old West Dock alongside a loading clay boat. c.1920s. The Royal Naval Voluntary Reserve was formed in 1903, replacing a similar earlier organisation. After the First World War the Royal Naval Reserve took some time to re-establish itself. In 1921 the Edinburgh Division was allocated the aging WWI Monitor M23, which was renamed HMS Claverhouse, and based in the Old West Dock in Leith. At the outbreak of the Second World War,

the Royal Naval Volunteer Reserve moved to the former Granton Hotel in Granton Square, where it remained until the savage defence cuts of 1994. The former Shore Base is now home to the Field Hospital Volunteers and both the Army and Sea Cadets.

The crew of HMS *Claverhouse* at the West Old Dock c.1922, posing in front of what may well be trophies won for marksmanship. The training ship paid particular attention to gunnery training, which perhaps explains the display of the light gun in the photo.

Leith Nautical College. (*above*)
Situated in Commercial Street
opposite the junction with Admiralty
Street, Leith Nautical College started
life in Mariners Church in Commercial
Street in 1855. After moving between
several premises including Dock Place
and Tollbooth Wynd, a permanent
home was eventually secured in
Commercial Street in 1903, where it
remained for the following 74 years.
In the early years boys as young as
10 years old who had ambition to
become professional seamen learned
basic seamanship skills at the College.
In later years classes were expanded to
cover instruction in engineering or
navigation. Throughout the years Leith
Nautical College was responsible for
training literally thousands of young men,
many of them going on to carve out a
successful career in the merchant navy,
several reaching a rank of distinction.
In 1977 the college moved to premises
in Milton Road, now home to Jewel

and Esk College. Today, in Scotland,
the task of training young potential
merchant seamen now lies in the hands
of Glasgow Nautical College, but few
could dispute the important part played
by Leith Nautical College throughout
the years in the Port's illustrious
maritime history.

Leith Nautical College c.1920s.

SECTION 5
LEITH WALK, EAST TO BERNARD STREET

Leith Walk at Pilrig. Before the amalgamation with Edinburgh in 1920, the junction of Pilrig Street and Leith Walk marked the southernmost boundary of Leith. This photograph appears to have been taken in the late 1920s. Just to the right of the photograph is the Boundary Bar (now City limits) which lay directly in the path of the official extremity of the port. The actual boundary cut through the centre of the bar and it is said that, with the Edinburgh licensing laws allowing 30 minutes more drinking time than Leith at that time, customers would simply move from one end of the bar to the other for the extra 30 minutes. The empty gap on the left is now partly occupied by a Scotmid Co-operative store. In the centre of the photo is the distinctive steeple of Pilrig St Paul's Church. Opened on 13 August 1843, the church still plays an important

part in the community with thriving youth sections, including Anchor Boys, Boys' Brigade, Brownies and Guides.

Leith Walk at the corner of Dalmeny Street probably around 1910. (*overleaf*) The open-topped electric tram on the left of the photo has just left the terminus at Pilrig. Leith was far ahead of Edinburgh as far as trams were concerned, moving from horse-drawn cars to electricity in 1905. The Edinburgh system was of the cable type, a less reliable system, which was later prone to breakdown and delays. Unfortunately, passengers wishing to travel from Leith to Edinburgh were required to change at what was termed the 'Pilrig muddle' because of the different track layouts. After the amalgamation of Leith and Edinburgh in 1920, both systems would revert to electricity, allowing a journey

between both Burghs to be accomplished uneventfully. The first journey on the new Edinburgh all electric line went from Pilrig to Fairmilehead via Princess Street in 1922.

Sloan Street. With houses on only the one side, Sloan Street runs between Dalmeny Street and Lorne Street. The former Iona Street park is in the foreground. Purchased in 1891 as a showground with rented booths and stalls, there would be regular visits by carnivals and circuses, and it is said that the first moving pictures to be seen in

Leith were shown on the site in a standing-only booth. It has now been renamed Dalmeny Street Park and contains both a swing park and a bowling green, both extensively used by excitable noisy children and the sometimes equally excitable and noisy bowlers.

The Alhambra Picture House in Leith Walk c.1960s. Situated on the corner of Leith Walk and Jane Street, the Alhambra opened as a theatre on 28 December 1914. Among the many proud boasts in advertising at the time were claims made of its electric vacuum system,

portable fire extinguishers and 15-piece orchestra. Among the many celebrities who have appeared in the theatre throughout the years have been Jack Anthony, the comedian Dave Willis senior, Yorkshire lass Gracie Fields, who made her first Edinburgh appearance in the theatre in 1920, leader of the Crazy Gang Bud Flanagan, and Leith's own boxer Tancy Lee. Later converted into a picture house, the Alhambra fell victim to the general recession caused in no little way by the increasing popularity of television, and closed its doors for the last time on 8 March 1958. The premises lay boarded up for many years until it was finally demolished in 1974. The two ornate lamp standards that stood outside the premises featuring the Leith coat-of-arms were believed to have been the only privately-owned street lamps in the entire city.

View of Easter Road and the corner of Albion Road at around 1910. (*above*) The corner of Albion

Road in the photograph was just outside the Leith boundary at that time. The low building on the left is the booking office of the North British Railway's Easter Road Station that opened in 1895 and was in service until it closed in 1947. Although the occasional excursion special still uses the line, the station buildings are long gone. Most of the crowd appear to occupy the one side of the street with several more making their way from Albion Road, suggesting that a game involving Hibernian Football Club had just taken place at Easter Road Stadium, which is a few hundred yards or so out of the picture. The first Hibs Easter Road ground, occupied by the club between the years 1880–1891, was situated down a lane from the main street just behind the tall tenement on the left.

Easter Road at Albion Road. (*overleaf*) A reverse view of the previous photograph showing the junction of Easter Road and Albion Road at around the same time. The Leith boundary was

only a few yards down Easter Road itself, roughly along the lines of the opening second right that led to the Eastern Cemetery. A wall just a few yards along Albion Road, on the right of the photo, still sports a small plaque bearing the simple inscription 'E/L', informing the curious that this spot marks the boundary between Edinburgh and Leith.

Easter Road Stadium and the Hibernian side of 1915. Part of the ground including the grandstand in the background lay just inside the Leith

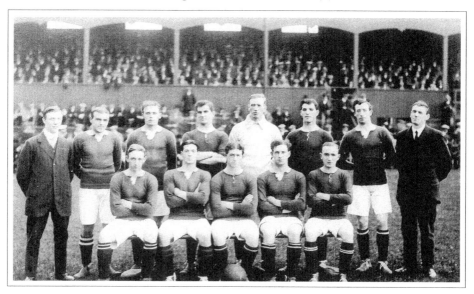

boundary. Moving to the site of the present Easter Road in 1893, the stadium at various times has been completely or partly inside the Leith perimeter depending on the changing extremities. Although formed in the heart of Edinburgh in 1875, Hibernian are now considered by many to be a Leith team and have fairly recently incorporated the Leith Persevere emblem as part of their current badge.

A game between Hibernian and city rivals Hearts at Easter Road, at around 1930. The grandstand featured in the previous photo was on the east side of the ground, but was dismantled in 1924 when a new main or centre stand was constructed directly opposite. The area previously occupied by the old grandstand was converted to terracing at the same time and can be seen in the background of the photo. An extension to the terracing was added in 1949 and 1950, and this helped to accommodate 65,840 spectators for a game between

Hibs and Hearts on 2 January 1950, which is still the largest crowd to have watched a football match in the city and one of the few times that the attendance for an Edinburgh derby was bigger than an 'Old Firm' game played on the same day. The gates had been closed ten minutes or so before the start, with several thousands outside still clamouring for admission. Meanwhile, many who had already paid left the ground before the kick-off, complaining of being unable to even see the pitch. Such was the crush that two people were known to have died, one at the game itself, the other shortly after arriving home.

View of Easter Road near the junction of Lorne Street on the left and St Clair Avenue on the right c.1920s. (*overleaf*) The pub on the corner would later be owned by the famous Hibs and Celtic goalkeeper Ronnie Simpson. The railway bridge crossing the street in the distance at the junction of Thorntree Street formed part

of the Caledonian Railway line which ran from Newhaven to Seafield, and which also crossed the busy roads at Bonnington Toll and Leith Walk. This bridge is not to be confused with the railway bridge that was situated near the foot of Easter Road, which formed part of the North British Railway system from Leith Central Station. Because of the low height of this latter bridge and the rail bridge over Abbeymount ,a short distance away, the circular No. 1 bus route was of necessity a single decker. Both bridges over Easter Road are now

long gone, with the one at the foot of Easter Road remaining until the 1970s.

Lochend Road School. (*below*) Situated near the junction of Easter Road and diagonally opposite what was once the Leith Academy Secondary, Lochend Road School opened its doors to pupils in January 1887 as a replacement for an earlier primary school in Portland Road. The official opening ceremony was performed by the Edinburgh University Principal, Sir William Muir. Closed several years ago, it has now been converted into flats.

Hermitage Park forms part of the southern end of Lochend Road. (*top right*) Hermitage Park Primary School is off to the right behind the distant tenements. The entrance to Beechwood Park, home of Leith Athletic Football Club between 1890 and 1899, was just off to the left of the photograph. The club was forced to look for a new

ground, one of many that they would occupy throughout the years, when the land was required as part of the new railway line from Leith Central Station to Waverley in 1903.

Leith Athletic were surely the most travelled of all Edinburgh's senior football teams. Formed in 1887, the club had a chequered history. Elected to the Scottish League in 1910 as a replacement for Cowlairs, who had finished the previous season rock bottom, the club fared reasonably well in its first season, and finishing fifth in a 12-team league.

Relegated after finishing second bottom in 1894-95, in place of bottom club Dumbarton, after a vote, they were replaced in the top division by the recently reformed Hibernian. During the following ten seasons, the club managed to finish a more than respectable second on four different occasions and were fourth three times, but that was not enough to prevent them from being wound up at the end of season 1904-05. Reformed the following year, and now named simply 'Leith FC', the club won the Second Division championship at the first time of asking, again failing to be elected into the First Division. Demonstrating just how difficult it must have been to keep the club afloat, during its 66 year history Leith Athletic had a grand total of 10 home grounds, which a return to several. Again restored to their original name, Athletic managed to win the Championship again in 1909-10, but for a third time were deprived of a place in the top division after a vote. The club

LEITH'S RECORD. DOUBLE CHAMPIONSHIP FLAGS 1905-1906
LEITH V ALBION ROVERS. 25TH AUGT 1906. RESULT 2-1 FOR LEITH

disbanded in 1916 during the First World War, but again took its place in the Scottish League when they joined the Second Division in time for the 1927–28 season, finishing 13th. Their only appearance in the First Division came in 1929–30, when they were promoted as champions but after only two seasons in the top division they returned to the lower league once more. Disbanded during the Second World War, they were elected to the Second Division in 1947 and playing at Meadowbank. Their first game was a friendly against Rangers, but the club folded completely in 1953. The game which saw them defeat Albion Rovers to win the Championship in 1906 was played at the Second Logie Green, the site now partly occupied by the B&Q car park and warehouse and the former premises of the well-known printing firm George Waterston's in Warriston Road, who ceased trading in 2003 after 251 years in the city.

The 1896 Scottish Cup Final between Hibs and Hearts was played at the first Logie Green, home ground of St Bernard's, which was situated just a few yards from where the photo was taken. It remains the only occasion to date that a Scottish Cup Final has been played outside of Glasgow.

Looking east along Restalrig Road towards Restalrig Village c.1920s. The low building in the centre of the photograph was used for a time as a Post Office, but at the time of writing it is empty and up for sale. A few yards out of the picture on the left was the well-known local hostelry, The Learig. Although the buildings in the photo remain almost the same, the absence of cars makes the same scene so different today.

On 27 August 1784, John Tytler, editor of the second and third editions of the *Encyclopaedia Britannica*, became the first person in this country to travel more

than half a mile by balloon. Influenced by similar flights then taking place in France, Tytler decided to make his own attempt. Taking off from the Comely Gardens leisure park near London Road, he reached a height of over 300 feet before eventually landing safely in the Restalrig area ten minutes later. Some record books credit the first flight to James Sadler of Oxford, but Tyler's flight took place a full six weeks before Sadler took to the air.

A still-to-be-properly-surfaced East Restalrig Terrace in the early years of the century. (*top*) Blackie Road is in the distance, the two streets divided by Restalrig Road at the high tenements.

Leith Links from Restalrig Road late 1920s. As one of the early homes of golf, Leith Links played a prominent part in the history of the town. It is said that in a desperate measure to prevent the public from crossing the course when games were taking place, the members of the golf club created a path that divided

the east and west links. The move proved pointless, as the path was mainly ignored by the townsfolk, but in time it was developed into a proper road and named Links Gardens. During the great Bubonic Plague of 1645 many of the infected citizens had been housed in wooden huts erected on the East Links in an attempt to prevent the spread of the disease that claimed the lives of more than half the population, and many of the dead are believed to have been buried in the immediate area. For many years, Leith Franklin Cricket Club have played their home games on the East Links, and at one time the annual Leith versus Edinburgh challenge match was eagerly awaited, as was the yearly pre-season charity game

LEITH LINKS. (71)

against local side Hibernian, which usually drew a large crowd. The money raised from the collection would be presented to the nearby Eastern Hospital.

The Bandstand at Leith Links
c.1904. The headquarters of the Scottish Wholesale Cooperative Society, founded in 1877 in Links Place, is in the right background, easily identified by its huge clock tower. In the early years of the last century listening to music on the Links was a popular pastime, particularly on Saturday evenings and Sunday afternoons. Regular free concerts would be held, often featuring military bands. It was near the bandstand just before the War that the famous Leith policeman, Willie Merrilees, who was born just off the Kirkgate and would later achieve the rank of Chief Constable, caught a man who had been molesting young women in the area, by hiding in a pram pushed by a policewoman posing as a nanny. In his time, Merrilees was perhaps Scotland's most famous policeman. Despite being only 5 feet 6 inches tall, well below the accepted height for enlistment, and having lost the fingers of his left hand, the young Merrilees so impressed the Chief Constable with his determined attitude that he was allowed to join the force, and quickly climbed through the ranks. In his youth, Merrilees rescued so many people from drowning in Leith Docks that it was

suggested, perhaps only jokingly, that he must have pushed them in himself. In 1933 he was involved in the famous raid on the Kosmo Club, a well-known brothel in Cathedral Lane in the city centre, and on 30 September 1940 he arrested the German spy Werner Wälti near the lost luggage department of Waverley Station. Wälti was subsequently hanged along with fellow conspirator Karl Drude in Wandsworth Prison in London on 6 August 1941.

An old engraving of golfers on Leith Links taken from Grants *Old and New Edinburgh* c.1880s. As can be seen, the terrain was vastly different from that of today, then rough and uneven. Note also the drying washing and the public walking freely throughout the area as a game of golf was taking place. The first recorded mention of golf on the Links was in 1457 when King James II banned the game because it was taking up time that should have been used practising archery, and in 1592 the Church of Scotland prohibited the game from being played on a Sunday, because it encouraged the parishioners to miss the church sermons.

The Links has played a major part in the history of the port. As already mentioned, today the area bears absolutely no relation to the Links of the Middle Ages. Sold to Edinburgh by Mary Queen of Scots in the 1500s, the area returned to Leith after independence in 1833, and it was eventually purchased from the city in 1856 for £650.

In earlier years the grassy overgrown and uneven ground stretched northwards to Leith Sands, eastwards as far as Seafield, and also took in large parts of Restalrig and Lochend. As well as golf, the area

had always been a popular place of recreation, used for military practice, grazing cattle, bleaching clothes, horse riding, cock fighting, duelling, and bowling, amongst other things, and at one time it had even sported a boating pond. On several occasions throughout the years armies had camped on the Links. The two large earthen mounds in the park, Giant's Brae and Lady Fife's Brae, were at one time thought to have been used as gun emplacements during the siege of Leith in 1560, although this is now not thought to be the case. For a while in the 19th century an Observatory was even situated on top of Giant's Brae, and remains of the foundations can still be seen. In 1778, only a year before the mutiny on the shore which ended in tragic circumstances, another military standoff that could well have had more serious consequences took place on the Links. The Seaforth Highlanders, who had been stationed at Edinburgh Castle, were ordered to Leith to embark for foreign service. There was major unrest amongst the ranks, many complaining of poor treatment by the officers and of failing to receive their wages. Rumours also abounded that they had been sold to the East India Company, and on reaching Leith Links half of their number, about 500 men, mutinied, steadfastly refusing to go any further. Because the soldiers were well armed it was not thought wise to challenge them with force, and they were allowed to march to the top of Arthur's Seat, where they constructed a simple defensive wall, the remains of which can still be seen. The men were fed by sympathetic townsfolk and serenaded from below by a lone piper; the area to this day is still called 'Pipers Walk'. After three days, an agreement was finally reached, and they marched to the harbour before embarking on service in the Channel Islands.

The first golf tournament in the world exclusively for professionals took place on Leith Links on 14 May 1867. Although the origins of the game are lost in the mists of time, it is believed that it first had its roots in Scotland, with Leith Links playing a prominent part as one of the earliest courses. In 1744, the regulations for the world's first recorded golf tournament were said to have been written in Luckie Clephan's tavern on the west side of the Kirkgate. A silver golf club was to be presented to the winner by The City of Edinburgh as first prize. In the Council minutes from the time, only six lines were devoted to discussing the forthcoming trip to Edinburgh by Johnny Cope, who was to be made a Freeman of the city, while almost three pages were dedicated to the rules of golf. The rules would be amended several times throughout the years to take account of the many different regulations used by each individual club, but in time the amended laws would be adopted by The Royal and Ancient Company of Golfers, who had moved to St Andrews in 1777. These are now the accepted regulations throughout the world. In 1768 just under two dozen members of the Honourable Edinburgh Company of Golfers each subscribed £30 in order to purchase a clubhouse, which was situated at the 'south west corner of the Links near the foot of Easter Road', and believed to be the first such venture in the world. Originally, the Leith competition was for players of all backgrounds, but after a protest to the town Council, it was agreed that only noblemen and gentlemen could become members, and the name changed to simply The Honourable Company of Golfers. In 1831 changes to the landscape made the five-hole Links course less popular with the players, and a gradual fall in membership necessitated the sale of the clubhouse. Five years later the Honourable Company moved, first to Musselburgh, where there was an eight hole course, before finally settling at Muirfield, where they remain to this day.

In the photograph, young Tom Morris is on the extreme right next to his father, Tom.

Professional Golfers at Leith Links, 14 May 1867. (*below*) Old Tom Morris is in front of the railings on the right; Morris Junior at the rear.

Leith Academy. (*right*) Founded by South Leith Parish Church to replace an earlier grammar school in the town, and possibly built on or near the site of some of the burial pits for victims of the great plague of 1650, who were said to have been interred in the south west corner of the Links, the present Leith Academy building dates from 1906. Originally for pupils of all ages, the

school became overcrowded in the late 1920s and a new secondary school was erected in Duke Street in 1931. The new school was built on the site of what had been Watts Hospital, the hospital itself believed to have been built on the site of the original golf clubhouse in 1862. The new secondary school moved to more modern premises just off Easter Road in 1991 and the Duke Street site is now occupied by St Margaret's College.

Front view of the first Leith Academy c.1900s.

The Academy and gardens pictured from Academy Street, again at the beginning of the century. The gardens have also been identified by some historians as a possible site of the burial pits for the victims of the great plague that swept through the area with such devastating results in 1650.

Duke Street looking West c.1910. The foot of Easter Road is just out of the photo on the left; the opening to

Academy Street on the right. One of the buildings on the left is the Golf Tavern, which, as the name implies, has a long association with the game. The Duke's Head public house is in the middle distance. Once owned by the well-known 1960s Rangers and Scotland player, Jimmy Miller, it had also been owned in the early years of last century by the Hibs chairman, Phillip Farmer, a great uncle of Sir Tom Farmer. Again, the camera has proved a popular diversion, particularly with the children, many of whom are in bare feet. Despite the construction of Leith Central Station in 1903 and its subsequent demolition in the 1990s, the area in the photograph remains largely unchanged today.

Wellington Place looking towards the Links. (*below*) The steeple of St Paul's Church in Constitution Street can be seen in the background. The area was badly damaged by fire in the late 1970s, although fortunately the church survived. Private housing now occupies the site of the fire. The outline of the Nestle's Milk sign can still be seen on the light coloured warehouse on the left.

The Council Chambers. (*overleaf top*) Located at the corner of Constitution Street and Queen Charlotte Street, the Council Chambers were opened in 1828. As well as the Council Chambers,

the building also housed Leith Police Station, which was extended in 1864, complete with cells (the small two storey building on the left) and a courtroom. In 1837 it became the headquarters of the Leith Fire Brigade until it moved to more modern premises in Junction Place in 1878, becoming part of the Edinburgh Fire Brigade after the amalgamation in 1920. Today the building is used solely as a police station, although the courtroom and former debating chamber can still be visited.

Another view of the Council Chambers. (*below*) The spire of St Johns Free Church is on the left. The church, with its 130 foot high tower which, at one time, sported a giant clock, was opened 27 June 1870 at a cost of £7,500. Closed as a place of worship many years ago, it has been occupied by several businesses, including at one time the local firm Leith Glazing. Like many other historic buildings in the town, it has now been converted into private housing.

Horse-drawn tram at the junction of Constitution Street and Bernard Street in the early 1890s. (*overleaf*) The Assembly Rooms are on the right, adjacent to the Exchange buildings. In the right background separated by Baltic Street is the Corn Exchange, its west exterior wall still displaying a beautiful ornamental frieze depicting the many trades that were once important to the port. A few hundred yards along Baltic Street can be found Salamander Street,

Burns' Monument, Corn Exchange and Assembly Rooms, Leith.

the scene of a potentially serious, but otherwise mildly humorous, incident, known thereafter as the Battle of Salamander Street. During the Second World War an anti-submarine minefield was in place between Inchkeith Island and Leith. One day, observers on the island noticed a British trawler about to enter the minefield. Failing to alert the ship's attention to the danger, a dummy warning shot was fired across its bows. However, because of the low trajectory, the shell ricocheted off the water like a stone on a pond, and proceeded to pass straight through a top flat of a tenement in Salamander Street, finally coming to rest in Loganlea, badly damaging another house. Fortunately no one was seriously injured in the incident and it is said that the projectile was later returned to the battery on Inchkeith. Fortifications on Inchkeith had protected Leith and the upper reaches of the Forth for centuries, the island at various times in the hands of the English and French. Now home to a

fully automatic and modern lighthouse, the island's first warning light for shipping had been erected as early as 1803.

View of the Corn Exchange building at the junction of Constitution Street and Baltic Street c.1911. (*overleaf*) The Assembly Rooms and Exchange Buildings are on the right. In the 19th century the foot of the street would be open to Leith Sands and the sea, and it is said that the last two men to be convicted of piracy in this country were hanged near this spot in January 1823. Throughout the years many executions had been carried out at the sands. The first recorded instance occurred in 1551, when several of the victims were chained below the high water mark, leaving the rising tide to carry out the gruesome sentence. Before the bridge was constructed at the Shore which allowed trains to cross the river, the area near the foot of Constitution Street was the final

destination for the many horse-drawn wagons that brought coal to Leith from mines in the Lothians. From there, the coal would be transported to the docks by horse-drawn cart. The Burns Statue by David Stevenson was erected in 1898 by the Robert Burns Appreciation Society. It eventually proved a major obstacle to traffic and has since been moved a few yards into Bernard Street.

The Leith Assembly Rooms
c.1900s. For many years the Assembly Rooms was a particularly popular location for dances, weddings, birthdays, and a multitude of other events, including its use at one time for a short spell as a picture house. Today the building has been turned into flats. At the corner of Mitchell Street between the Assembly Rooms and the Council Chambers lay the Leith Post Office. Opened in 1876, it closed during the 1970s.

The south side of Bernard Street
c.1900s showing the rounded frontage of what was originally the headquarters of the Leith Bank, which was founded in 1793. The company moved to premises

at 20 Bernard Street at the beginning of the 19th century and later merged with the Edinburgh Savings Bank. Today the building is occupied by a computer software company.

Burns Statue and Bernard Street c.1906. The round dome of what was the headquarters of the Leith Bank is on the left. In the middle distance can be seen the entrance to Timber Bush. At one time, Timber Bush, or 'Bourse', was open to the sea and was used as a storage area for the colossal amount of timber that arrived each year at the port. Described as 'a large open space surrounded by a high wooden fence', it was used almost exclusively for the sale of timber. In the days of wooden ships, timber was a very valuable commodity and used extensively by many of the shipbuilding businesses that operated in the area. The Carriers Quarters public house is located just a few yards beyond the opening to Timber Bush. For many years, as the name would suggest, the Carriers Quarters was a popular

watering hole for many of the carters and sailors who plied their trade in Leith. The pub still retains a small cubicle called the Tulip Room, in which it is said many a financial transaction took place between businesswomen of the night and their potential customers. In 1845, Bernard Street was the starting point for the first ever horse-drawn tram journey from Leith to Haymarket in Edinburgh via Constitution Street, Leith Walk and Princes Street. Another occasion that excited the citizens of Leith was the return of the colossal cannon, Mons Meg, which had been taken to the Tower of London in 1754. After protests from many eminent figures in the capital, including Sir Walter Scott, the huge artillery piece was returned to Edinburgh in 1829. Unloaded at the shore amidst great excitement from the locals, the cannon was drawn by six black horses and made its way along Bernard Street, Constitution Street and Leith Walk, back to its rightful home in Edinburgh Castle, where it remains to this day.

SECTION 6 GREAT JUNCTION STREET
TO NORTH FORT STREET

Great Junction Street looking west.
The opening to Bonnington Road is on
left, alongside the advert for the then-
popular Buttercup Dairy, which adorns
the corner wall. At one time, the
Buttercup Dairy had a large refrigerated
storage warehouse at the foot of Easter
Road, leading to Hibs fans being taunted
that that was the only cup to be seen at
Easter Road. The Clock Tower of the
Leith Provident Cooperative Society,
erected in 1911, dominates the middle
distance of the photo; Leith Provident
opened its first ever shop in Great
Junction Street in May 1878. The building
on the immediate right of the photograph
is the St James Episcopal Hall, which was
demolished to make way for a modern
Leith Provident Grocery and Furniture
Store in the 1960s.

**The entrance to Leith Hospital in
Mill Lane at the turn of last
century**. Leith Hospital had perhaps a
unique claim to fame. Since it was first
opened in 1851, the sick children of the
town had been treated in adult wards in
the hospital, but it was later decided that
as soon as the Great War was over that
the building of a specialised children's
wing should be made a priority. During
the First World War, one sixth of the

population of the town had enrolled for military service, and of 14,000 men, 2205 made the ultimate sacrifice. Lord Provost Lindsay suggested that perhaps a new hospital wing could also become Leith's war memorial to the fallen. In less than a year, public subscription, including many generous donations from prominent businessmen, raised over £65,000, and the new children's wing in Taylor Gardens was officially opened on 29 January 1927 by the Secretary of State for Scotland, Sir John Gilmour. Ornate sculptures adorned the outside of the building, including the arms of the Royal Scots, who had lost many men in the Gretna Disaster, with representations from the other services who had served so gallantly during the conflict. A panel inside the building still commemorates the citizens of the town who fell during both World Wars.

Great Junction Street looking towards Junction Bridge. The tenements on the left and the adjacent

Ballantyne Street, which lay just behind, would be demolished in the 1970s.
The building on the right would be swept away during the 1930s to make way for the Art Deco style State Picture House, which first opened its doors in December 1938; the proceeds from the opening night went towards the nearby Leith Hospital. One of the features on the first night was 'Boots and Saddles', starring the legendary cowboy actor Gene Autrey. Both the Picture House and the adjacent Eldorado Ballroom, or 'The Eldo' as it was more popularly known, were built on the site of the disused Hawthorns Ship Building and Engineering Works, which backed onto the river.
In the left middle distance an electric tram appears to be picking up passengers outside the booking office for the Junction Bridge Station, the platform of which lay on a lower level. The station, part of the North British Railway system, was opened as Junction Road Station in 1869 but renamed Junction Bridge in 1923. It was here that Czar Nicholas II

departed for the Balmoral during his visit to Leith in 1896. The station, which was slightly damaged by a German bomb that fell on nearby Largo Place and the Town Hall in 1941, closed for the last time in 1947.

Great Junction Street from the top of North Junction Street at around the turn of the century. (*above*) The low building on the right is the booking office of Junction Bridge Station. The tenements in the background are long gone, as is the large building on the left which was part of the Hawthorn Works.

Junction Bridge and river from the top floor of a tenement at the corner of Ferry Road. The booking office for Junction Bridge Station is in the foreground. The photograph shows the bridge, built in 1818, before it was widened in 1903. Hawthorns Shipbuilding and Engineering Works are on the right. The depth of the water further up river from the harbour always restricted the

size of ships that could be built or repaired at Hawthorns and neighbouring yards. Consequently, three slipways of different sizes were located on the north side of the Hawthorns yard, all constructed at an angle to make launching much easier, considering the confines of the river at that point. Morton and Co., who designed the patent slip here in 1818, had premises on the opposite side of the river just south of the North Leith Burial ground. The ingenious Patent Slip consisted of a heavy steel frame that could be lowered on rails to rest below the keel of a ship. As the tide receded the ship would

gradually come to rest on the steel frame, which could then be winched from the river. The patent slipway allowed ships to be drawn from the water for repair, therefore avoiding the need for a graving dock. Much cheaper, and providing a cleaner environment in which to work, the system proved so popular that it was soon purchased by many other ship building and repair yards both in this country and abroad, including, it is said, as far as Russia. Although nothing remains today of this yard, a slight cut in the riverbank just south of the burial ground still identifies its location. The North Leith burial ground, which contains the remains of many of the old town's worthies, including the grandfather of the Liberal Prime Minister, William Gladstone, can be seen in the middle distance in front of the premises of Bell's the seed merchants. This building would later be better known as McGregor's Quayside Mills, but has since been converted into flats.

North Junction Street photographed from the foot of Ferry Road, looking towards the docks c.1912. On the left, behind the hay cart, was the Scandinavian Lutheran Church that served the many foreign seamen who visited the port, and is now home to the Leith School of Art. David Kilpatrick's School, or DK's as it was commonly known, was a little further down on the same side. Built at the beginning of the Great War, the school building was quickly turned into an army barracks until the cessation of hostilities. Slightly damaged by the bombs that also caused such devastation to the Town Hall and Largo Place in 1941, the school remains in the affections of the thousands of pupils who attended throughout the years before its eventual closure in the 1970s. Used latterly by the sea cadets, the building has since been demolished and the site is now a play area for young children.

The corner of Coburg Street is on the right, with the Admiralty Street opening a

little further down. The well-known Tod's Mills was situated in the far distance at the corner of Commercial Street, opposite the west entrance to the docks. The Mill fell victim to one of the many serious fires that have occurred in Leith throughout the years in April 1885. A few years later, six people, including two children, died after a serious explosion at the factory.

The Foot of Ferry Road from the top of Coburg Street. (*below*)

The area behind the brick wall on the right hand side would become the site of the new Leith Town Hall and Library. Erected on land previously belonging to the manse of North Leith Church, work started on the Town Hall in 1929 and it was officially opened in July 1932. On 7 April 1941 the surrounding area fell prey to German bombs, which caused severe damage to the building. Restoration to the original design began in 1955 and both the Town Hall

and Library were officially reopened 23 June 1961. The spire of St Ninian's Church in Ferry Road is in the background.

The foot of Ferry Road at the junction of both North and Great Junction Streets. (*below*) The Corner

Rooms on the left was another popular private function suite for weddings and other events. Coburg Street lies behind the tramcar. Both the Corner Rooms and the shops at the corner of Junction Bridge in the right background are now long gone.

Ferry Rd. Leith.

Junction Mills and the Water of Leith from Junction Bridge. The large building in the background is Junction Flour Mills. A mill had stood on the spot for centuries, originally owned by the Logan's. Latterly it was the site of one of the two flour mills in the area belonging to the Scottish Cooperative Wholesale Society. The other was Chancelot Mills, whose clock tower can just be made out in the right distance. Both closed in 1967 when new modern premises were opened on reclaimed land at the West Harbour. The platform and rail track of Junction Bridge Station can be seen on the right, including the banking that was slightly damaged during the same German raid that damaged the Town Hall. The station was extremely

lucky to escape so lightly, for some of the buildings in nearby Largo Place were extensively damaged. Fortunately, there was no loss of life. The slip of Beaumont & Co shipbuilders is on the left. Although nothing remains today of the yard itself, the concrete slipway can still be seen.

Ferry Road at Dudley Avenue. (*above*) The corner of Trafalgar Street is on the left; the Junction of Ferry Road and Newhaven Road in the middle distance. It was along Ferry Road in 1827 that Timothy Burstal, working from 'Leith Mills' and described as 'a man of no ordinary scientific knowledge and skill', first tested his experimental steam engine. The engine named 'Perseverance' was taken to Rainhill, just outside Manchester,

on 14 October 1829 to compete against three other steam engines for a £500 prize. Unfortunately, the engine was damaged in transit and did not take part in the trials, and although he was commended for his invention, the first prize went to Stevenson's 'Rocket'; the rest, as they say, is history.

Summerside Place in the early years of last century. (*bottom left*) The view is greatly changed from today, with not a single motor car to be seen. The church in the background has since been demolished.

The Scottish Cooperative Chancelot Flour Mill c.1900s. (*below*) Opened on 24 August 1894, the Mill was described at the time as a most impressive example of architecture. Its huge clock tower was a landmark which could be seen for miles.

Like its near neighbour, Junction Mills, Chancelot would be in operation for 73 years, until making way for the modern Chancelot Mill at Leith Docks in the late 1960s. The building lay derelict for a few years, until it was badly damaged by fire and demolished in 1971. A modern housing estate now occupies the site. For many years approximately 40 tons of flour would be transported daily by lorry from Chancalot to an emergency government storage facility at Innerleithen. Four lorry loads of rotated stock would then be returned to the mill each day.

Ferry Road looking east c.1920. The tram has just passed the junction of South and North Fort Streets on its way

to Granton. The spire of the now demolished St Ninian's Church can be seen in the background. Except for the traffic and the church that was demolished in the 1970s, the scene remains much the same today.

Chancelot Terrace opposite the junction of Craighall Road and Ferry Road. (*below*) Chancelot Flour Mill can be seen in the right background. Chancelot Park, just one of the many home grounds of Leith Athletic, who played there between 1900 and 1904, and again in 1919 to 1924, is hidden between the terrace and the Mill.

The ground has now been renamed Letham Park, and the pitch is still used by football teams of the Boys' Brigade.

North Fort Street looking towards the river in the early years of the century. (*below*) During the Second World War, the area would be hit by an enemy bomb, leaving six people dead and several more injured in George Street (marked with a cross). Patrons who attended the Palace, State and Alhambra picture houses that night can still remember being alerted to the bombing by a notice on the screen advising anyone from the immediate area to return home at once.

Leith did not escape the attentions of the enemy during the First World War either. Just before midnight on 2 April 1916, the citizens of the town were alarmed to see the German Zeppelin L14 hovering over the port. Within minutes, nine high explosive shells and 11 incendiaries had been dropped on the town. The manse in

North Fort Street, Leith

Mill Lane was hit, as was a bonded warehouse at Ronaldson's Wharf on The Shore, causing almost £50,000 worth of damage. Unfortunately, a 66 year old man was later found dead in the street and a one year old boy had been killed while he slept. They were Scotland's first ever air raid victims. Because 'North Britain', as the Germans called it, had been thought to be well beyond the range of airships, there was little in the way of an anti-aircraft deterrent, and after attacking Leith the L14 proceeded in a leisurely fashion across the capital, dropping more bombs haphazardly in the city centre as it passed. It then made its escape over East Lothian to the North Sea, leaving behind another eight dead, including two children, and an additional 11 injured. In the same attack, L22 had dropped several bombs over Colinton and Liberton, thankfully without causing any casualties.

Leith Fort in the years immediately preceding the First World War. Many of the retaining walls have survived, including the guardroom and adjutant's office that can be seen just inside the gate, after the internal buildings were demolished in the 1960s to make way for Council housing. It was after the threat to Leith by the Scot, John Paul Jones, during the American Wars of Independence that it was decided to build a fort to protect the Port from any further attacks. In 1777, Jones, credited as being the Father of the American Navy, led three ships into the Forth and lay just off Inchkeith Island. An ultimatum was sent to the town fathers that, unless he received £200,000, an astronomical sum at the time, he would attack the Port. Fortunately, before any deal could be concluded, a huge gale swept the pirate and his fleet out to sea and the danger was averted. A local reverend was said to have approached the water's edge to pray for salvation

from the raider, and, whether this act was responsible or not, Leith was saved. The incident provoked the city leaders to build a nine gun fort to defend the town, and the work finished in 1780. At that time, the water's edge would be only a few yards from the walls of the Fort, giving the defenders an unimpeded view of the river, something difficult to imagine today with the many houses that have been built on land reclaimed from the sea. The Fort never did see action, the nearest being when it narrowly escaped the German Bombs which wreaked such damage to the area during the Second World War. At the time of writing, the houses inside the perimeter are now themselves under threat of demolition.

The Junction of North Fort Street and Lindsay Road looking toward Leith, showing Sinclair's Public House, also known as the Half Way House. The area is much changed today: the new road that bypassed the Main Street at Newhaven in the 1970s cut off the foot of North Fort Street from the heavy traffic. Then, the water's edge would have been only a few yards from the left of the photograph. In the far distance, behind the cart at the junction with Portland Street, tram traffic from Leith to Granton was once severely disrupted when a discarded Second World War German bomb created a great crater in the middle of the road. For a short time, until a repair could be made, passengers travelling between Leith and Granton would have to change trams at either side of the crater. Lindsay Road is named after the former Lord Provost, William Lindsay, who was largely responsible for improving much of the sub-standard housing and sanitation in the town. Then, the harbour area was particular susceptible to disease and the water strewn with putrid waste: the mortality rate of young children was unacceptably high. The passing of the Edinburgh and Leith Sewage Act in 1864 went some way in alleviating the problem.

SECTION 7 PILRIG TO NEWHAVEN

Leith Walk at the junction with Pilrig Street c.1904.

The 'Pilrig Muddle' c.1910. (*right*)
Leith was already well ahead of Edinburgh as far as public transport was concerned, with the first electric tram taking to the streets in 1905. At that time Edinburgh was at loggerheads with Leith and refused to embrace electricity, relying instead on the cable car system, which would be found to be unreliable and prone to regular breakdowns. Passengers wishing to travel from Leith to the city by tram were obliged to change from one tram to the other at the boundary at Pilrig. It became known as the Pilrig Muddle, and it was not until both changed to a unified electric tram system in 1922 that the problem was finally eradicated. The first journey for the new unified tram system left from Pilrig on its way to Fairmilehead that same year.

Mass funeral parade for soldiers killed in the Gretna Rail Disaster.

The Gretna Rail Disaster remains the country's heaviest loss of life in a train accident to this day. On 22 May 1915, a train containing soldiers of the 7th Royal Scots, a territorial regiment that had been raised in Leith, left Larbert on its way to Liverpool for embarkation to Gallipoli. As the troop train approached Quintenshill, not far from Gretna, it collided with a stationary local train standing on the main down line. Minutes later, the northbound Euston to Glasgow express ploughed through the wreckage of both trains adding further carnage to the scene. The troops had been travelling on ancient stock pressed into service which were lit by gas lamps, and soon the entire area was turned into a blazing inferno. Over 200 were killed in both the local and troop trains and a further 200 injured. At a roll call taken a short while later only 57 able-bodied men were capable of answer. The soldiers who were able, were initially sent on to Liverpool to continue their journey to Gallipoli, but thankfully reason prevailed, and the men were returned to their homes to recuperate. It later turned out that a signalman who was due to start work at six o' clock in the morning had an arrangement with the night man that he would start ten minutes later, allowing him to catch a lift to work on a local train. Because entries were required to be made in handwriting, any entry after six o' clock could not have been recorded by the night man, and train movements after this time were written on a slip of paper. The replacement was unaware that the local was still on the main line and sent the troops' transport forward to collide with the stationary train. Both men were later jailed for their part in the catastrophe. Many of the dead were given private funerals but over a hundred were buried in Rosebank Cemetery at Pilrig, the bodies lying overnight in the drill hall in Dalmeny Street. Later an impressive memorial was raised in Rosebank recording on several bronze panels the names of those who had died in the tragedy and were interred in the cemetery. Because the accident happened in wartime it was not widely reported, and it was not until the 1960s that many people became fully aware of just what had happened near the Scottish border on that awful morning.

The monument in the cemetery was sculpted by John Rhind, who also carved the Victoria Statue at the Foot of the Walk.

Pilrig House c.1900s. Situated halfway between Edinburgh and Leith in what was then open countryside, it is believed that Pilrig House was built on the site of an ancient fort. At that time, the house was surrounded by orchards and fields, a long tree-lined avenue at what is now Balfour Street connecting it to what would later become Leith Walk. Built by the wealthy merchant Gilbert Goodwin in 1638, the house changed owners many times over the years, including Lord Rosebery and James Balfour. Robert Louis Stevenson's grandfather, Louis Balfour Stevenson, was born in the house in 1777, and quite possibly his mother, Mary Balfour, who is known to have lived there. Robert Louis Stevenson is said to have based the house of Shaws in his novel *Kidnapped* on Pilrig House. In the book the hero David Balfour narrowly escapes being murdered by his uncle Ebenezer Balfour at the house. It was also mentioned in the sequel, *Catriona*. Acquired by the local authorities during the Second World War, and used among other things as a woman's hostel, the house fell into disrepair in the 1960s. Badly damaged by both vandalism and a serious fire, it was eventually rebuilt, almost to its original form, in 1984 and is now private flats.

Tram at Bonnington Toll c.1907, taken from Pilrig Street. (*overleaf*) The site of the old Tollhouse is on the right behind the 'special' tram making its

way to Leith Walk. The bridge was part of the Caledonian Railway line that carried traffic from Newhaven to Seafield. Newhaven Road can be seen in the background, winding its way to Ferry Road. The bridge itself was removed around the 1970s, leaving only the red brick supports. Both these supports have since been dismantled, and houses erected at the north west corner and commercial warehouses diagonally opposite.

Bonnington Toll looking into Bonnington Road c.1890s. Before the opening of Leith Walk, Bonnington Road was one of the main approaches into Leith from Edinburgh, with the traveller required to pay a toll to pass from one Burgh to the other. The money raised helped to maintain the new thoroughfare. The Tollhouse was demolished in the late 1800s to make way for the bridge carrying the Caledonian Railway line.

Tram at the bend in Newhaven Road c.1900. (*top right*) Bonnington Bridge is in the background. A road of sorts, and a bridge over the river linking Newhaven with the city, had been in place at this spot for hundreds of years, and it is recorded that King James IV made regular crossings in 1511 to watch progress on his flagship, 'The Great Michael', which was then being built at Newhaven. As early as the 12th century, Bonnington had been a thriving village that relied almost entirely on the nearby Water of Leith for its livelihood, for it supplied power for

the numerous mills and granaries that were located in the area. The last mill closed in 1967, and its buildings were demolished despite great public protest. Sadly little remains today of this once prosperous village, except for the 17th century mill house, and a water wheel to remind visitors of its once affluent past. The area is now home to several small industrial units and modern housing.

Bonnington Bridge in snow c.1890s. The stone bridge at this spot was first opened in 1812. It was widened in a joint operation between Edinburgh and Leith in 1902–03

Bonnington Bridge around the 1920s. The Bridge Bar is on the right. Closed for several years, at the time of writing the former public house had recently been the subject of great police interest when a major cannabis farm was discovered in the basement. The corner of Graham Street can be seen immediately behind the Bridge Bar.

it gave regular service between North Leith Station and Cannonmills for 100 years. It finally closed to passenger travel in 1947 although it was used for freight until the 1960s. The site of the rail line is now incorporated as part of the Water of Leith Walkway, but the station building and platforms are still to be seen.

A snow-covered Bonnington Bridge looking east around the turn of the century. The bridge is yet to be widened. The Bridge Bar is on the left, the tall chimney in the background pumping out waste from one of the many factories that worked the area.

Newhaven Road looking towards the junction with Ferry Road in the early years of last century. The opening of Pitt Street can be seen on right of photograph. Again, perhaps the most notable thing about the scene compared to today is the almost complete lack of traffic and the absence of parked vehicles. The billboards on the left of the photo inform the public of the times of the rail traffic that passed through Bonnington Road Station that lay directly below. The station opened in 1847 to become the busiest on the line, even busier than Leith Central Station after its opening in 1903, and apart from a two year spell during the Great War,

Bowlers in Victoria Park. Once the home of Richard Raimes, a partner in the well-known firm of Raimes Clark the manufacturing chemists, the park retained the name of its former owner until it changed to commemorate the Golden Jubilee of Queen Victoria in June 1887. Raimes Park was the site of the first recorded game of Association Football to be played in Edinburgh. At that time Association Football, or soccer, was played mainly in the west side of the country, Edinburgh still being a Rugby stronghold, but on 28 December 1873 two sides from Glasgow, Queens Park and Clydesdale, who saw themselves as missionaries spreading the new code throughout the land, played an exhibition game in the park. The game was watched by a crowd of a few hundred, and many of the spectators left to form their own teams including Brunswick, Hanover, White Star, 3rd Edinburgh Volunteer Rifles and, in time, Hibs and Hearts.

The Fountain in Victoria Park c.1900. The fountain was a gift to the town from the Leith Horticulture, Industrial and Sports Society. From the dress of the children, it would appear that the photograph was taken on a Sunday. Once again the novelty of the camera has drawn a crowd of inquisitive onlookers, particularly the overly curious small child at the front of the photo.

The swing park in Victoria Park around the turn of the century. The bandstand in the background was always a popular venue, particularly on Saturday and Sunday afternoons.

Trams in Newhaven Road c.1905. (*overleaf*) The photograph is believed to have been taken on the opening day of the electric line to Newhaven in 1905.

The event, accompanied by a festival in nearby Victoria Park, was eagerly anticipated, with crowds turning up in large numbers to witness what was then an historic moment for the area.

Trams near the Newhaven Road terminus looking east c.1906. (*below*) Note the convergence, or 'pinch', of the tramlines in the foreground that allowed the trams to change to a single line to enable them to navigate the narrow Stanley Road. For many years, Stanley Road was the terminus of the tram system until it

was moved several hundred yards away to the foot of Craighall Road.

An all-but-deserted Newhaven Road at the turn of the century.

Newhaven Road. (*top right*) The open-topped tram has just left the terminus at Stanley Road at the top left hand corner of the photo. The top of 'Whale Brae' and Hawthornvale are in the distance.

Cherrybank at Stanley Road. Apart from the trams, tramlines and the absence of cars, like many of the photographs taken at the time, the scene remains almost the same today. Again, the tramlines in both directions were 'pinched' into one, just before the junction to allow tram cars to cope with the narrow width of Stanley Road.

Stanley Road pictured from Newhaven Road c.1906.

FURTHER READING

I am indebted to the authors of several magnificent books on Leith, their knowledge of the Port far greater than my own. These sources include:

Cant, Malcolm; *Villages of Edinburgh: North Edinburgh*; John Donald Publishers; 1985.

Carswell, Arch; *The Port of Leith*; Leith Chamber of Commerce; 1937.

Grant, James; *Cassell's Old and New Edinburgh, Volumes 1–3*; Nabu Press; 2010.

Hunter, D.L.G; *Edinburgh's Transport: The Early Years*; Mercat Press; 1992.

Marshall, James Scott; *Old Leith at Work*; Edina Press; 1977.

McGowran, Tom; *Newhaven on Forth: Port of Grace*; John Donald Publishers; 1997.

Mowat, Sue; *The Port of Leith*; John Donald Publishers; 1997.

Stevenson, J.L; *The Last Trams: Edinburgh*; Wherewithal Books, 1986.

Valentine, David Stewart; *Leith at Random*; Porthole Publications; 2004.

Valentine, David Stewart; *Leith Lives*; Porthole Publications; 2007.

Wallace, Joyce M; *Traditions of Trinity and Leith*; John Donald Publishers, 1997.

Wallace, Joyce M; *Further Traditions of Trinity and Leith*; John Donald Publishers, 1997.

Some other books published by **LUATH** PRESS

Arthur's Seat: Journeys and Evocations

Stuart McHardy and Donald Smith
ISBN: 978-1-908373-46-5 PBK £7.99

 Arthur's Seat, rising high above the Edinburgh sky-line, is the city's most awe-inspiring landmark. Although thousands climb to the summit every year, its history remains a mystery, shrouded in myth and legend. The first book of its kind, *Arthur's Seat: Journeys and Evocations* is a salute to the ancient tradition of storytelling, guiding the reader around Edinburgh's famous 'Resting Giant' with an exploration of the local folklore and customs associated with the mountain-within-a-city.

Two of the city's leading storytellers have sifted through the centuries to compile the remarkable guide to Edinburgh's famous landmark.
EDINBURGH EVENING NEWS

Calton Hill: Journeys and Evocations

Stuart McHardy and Donald Smith
ISBN: 978-1-908373-85-4 PBK £7.99

 Following on from the success of *Arthur's Seat, the Journeys and Evocations* series continues with a look at the events and folklore surrounding Edinburgh's iconic Calton Hill. Standing only 338 ft (103m) high, this small hill offers a fascinating view of Edinburgh both literally and historically. The book brings together prose, poetry and photographic images to explore the Calton Hill's role in radical and nationalist politics through the centuries as well as taking a look at the buildings, philosophy and intrigue of a central part of Edinburgh's landscape.

A fascinating spotlight on the Hill's unique position in centuries of Edinburgh life.
EDINBURGH EVENING NEWS

Edinburgh Old Town: Journeys and Evocations

John Fee, with Stuart McHardy and Donald Smith
ISBN: 978-1-9100001-56-9 PBK £7.99

 *John Fee was a true story-telling artist, painting verbal pictures, setting off on digressions that turned out not to be digressions, moving effortlessly into a song or poem. He has uncovered little-known aspects of the Royal Mile along with long-forgotten characters who spring back to life through the storyteller's art.*

Following on from the acclaimed *Arthur's Seat* and *Calton Hill* volumes, this third instalment in the *Journeys and Evocations* series focuses on the extensive history and folklore surrounding Edinburgh's atmospheric Old Town. Take a vivid trip with John Fee through Edinburgh's Old Town as you've never seen it before, with this wonderful blend prose, poetry, photography and incredible stories from another era of one of Edinburgh's most renowned districts.

This is Scotland: A Country in Words and Pictures

Daniel Gray and Alan McCredie
ISBN: 978-1-910021-59-0 PBK £9.99

 A Scotsman and an Englishman, a camera and a notebook...

McCredie's lens and Gray's words search out everyday Scotland – a Scotland of flaking pub signs and sneaky fags outside the bingo, Italian cafés and proper fitba grounds. A nation of beautiful, haggard normality.

A flirty glance at a dozen areas around the country – setting off in Leith and making tracks to both Highlands and Borderlands... Searching through Scotland what did they hear? Laughter. What did they smell? Mainly chips. This book has uncovered a country that is lived and living. It's a refreshing journey which makes you wonder, what is Scotland to you?
THE SKINNY

Luath Press Limited

committed to publishing well written books worth reading

LUATH PRESS takes its name from Robert Burns, whose little collie Luath (*Gael.,* swift or nimble) tripped up Jean Armour at a wedding and gave him the chance to speak to the woman who was to be his wife and the abiding love of his life. Burns called one of 'The Twa Dogs' Luath after Cuchullin's hunting dog in Ossian's *Fingal*. Luath Press was established in 1981 in the heart of Burns country, and now resides a few steps up the road from Burns' first lodgings on Edinburgh's Royal Mile. Luath offers you distinctive writing with a hint of unexpected pleasures.

Most bookshops in the UK, the US, Canada, Australia, New Zealand and parts of Europe either carry our books in stock or can order them for you. To order direct from us, please send a £sterling cheque, postal order, international money order or your credit card details (number, address of cardholder and expiry date) to us at the address below. Please add post and packing as follows: UK – £1.00 per delivery address; overseas surface mail – £2.50 per delivery address; overseas airmail – £3.50 for the first book to each delivery address, plus £1.00 for each additional book by airmail to the same address. If your order is a gift, we will happily enclose your card or message at no extra charge.

Luath Press Limited
543/2 Castlehill
The Royal Mile
Edinburgh EH1 2ND
Scotland
Telephone: 0131 225 4326 (24 hours)
email: sales@luath.co.uk
Website: www.luath.co.uk